TIME MANAGEMENT

for Entrepreneurs & Professionals

How to turn
time into
Productivity

by **Abigail
Barnes**

Tonbo Group

Orders: **www.successbydesigntraining.com**

Enquiries: **enquiries@successbydesigntraining.com**

ISBN: 978-1-914408-31-1

First published in 2013 by Tonbo Group. This edition 2021

CONTENT

INTRODUCTION 5

About the book 6

How will it benefit the reader 6

PREFACE 7

TIME MANAGEMENT 9

HOW TO USE YOUR TIME MORE EFFECTIVELY 14

5 STEP PROCESS FOR

TURNING YOUR TIME INTO PRODUCTIVITY 16

Step 1 – Track your time 16

Step 2 – Analyse your results 21

Step 3 – What your results say about you 24

Step 4 – Time to take action (our agreement) 36

Step 5 – Turning time into profit 38

VOCABULARY – How to talk yourself successful 50

HEALTH & LIFESTYLE 52

TIME CONFIDENCE 56

THE 888 FORMULA 57

Rest 58

Activities 61

Work 63

TIME PLANNING 65

ACTION PLAN 74

BONUS TIME TIPS 81

Professional 81

Entrepreneur 82

ACKNOWLEDGEMENTS 84

CASE STUDY BIOGRAPHIES 85

ABOUT THE AUTHOR 88

INTRODUCTION

Q. Would you like to have more time?

Q. To learn the secret for how to have more time, and make the time you do have more productive?

Q. To say goodbye to overwhelm, anxiety and frustration and become the happiest and most confident time manager you know?

Q. To learn how to create daily focus time and avoid all the distractions?

Q. Are you prepared to do whatever it takes to create the lifestyle you want?

If you answered yes to any of these questions then read on – this is the book for you!!

You hold in your hands a book full of thought provoking challenges and uncomfortable truths. It contains exciting, life-enhancing and life-changing solutions to the age-old problem of never seeming to have enough time to do what you want, when you want, with the people you want to.

Welcome to the ultimate time management guide for entrepreneurs and professionals. This book has been designed to help you review your current approach to time management, to better understand the consequences of your beliefs and habits, accept the reasons for change and begin the journey to becoming a more confident time manager one step at a time!

'Your time is your most valuable commodity, use it or lose it!'
Abigail Barnes

ABOUT THE BOOK

This book will help you to review your current time management habits using our 5-step method and identify the activities that are 'stealing' your valueable time and sabotaging your productivity.

It will teach you how to create an action plan for your new way of living and working and require you commit to making changes that will benefit your business, career and life.

HOW WILL IT BENEFIT YOU?

Have you ever stopped and calculated the cost of the time you waste?

If you spend two hours a day scrolling through social media that equates to 43,800 hours, which is over 30 days a year, that's a month of lost time, depending on your intention while scrolling of course!

What could you achieve in your business, career or life from today if you were more intentional with your time?

Once you accept that your current time management habits are creating the life you have, and apply the strategies recommended in this book, you will experience first hand what can be achieved with your 24-hour day.

TIP - Visit www.successbydesigntraining.com to get access to more tips, tools and training.

TIME MANAGEMENT TIP
'Time Management = Freedom*'*

PREFACE

On the morning of 25 February 2012. I woke up in Boston, USA, where I had flown to on a work Business trip, with odd migraine like symptoms. 24 hours later I was in a hospital being told by a Doctor that I'd had a stroke and would be going to the intensive care unit, not to my meetings!

My name is Abigail Barnes, and prior to starting my business (Success by Design Training) in 2013, I worked in financial services marketing for Investment Managers, Asset Managers and Hedge Funds for over 10 years. This gave me a solid grounding in all areas of the marketing mix, stakeholder and shareholder management and it also enabled me to work with some of the best Fund Managers, agencies and suppliers in the world.

My interest in Time Management started at the dinner table age 4. This was where my Dad used to share stories with us about the projects he was involved in, for the local authorities he worked for at the time.

It grew when I went to Oxford Brookes University to study Business & Marketing Management. I loved every minute of my degree, the concepts, the city and the people I met. A few years into my career I studied evenings and weekends to get a professional postgraduate diploma in Marketing (CIM).

Life was a blur for a long time after my stroke. I'd been given a second chance but I didn't feel grateful I felt scared, numb and uncertain about every decision I had to make.

Now I knew what regret would feel like if I died not having made the most of this second chance, but nothing made sense anymore. I felt guilty, crazy and confused. All I wanted to do was sleep and hide.

Fast-forward a few years. What doesn't kill you really does make you stronger!

Now I was ready to maximise every moment. To create the work/life balance that I wanted, start the business I had always dreamed of and write a book. When life knocks you down get up as quickly as you can, and make rock bottom your solid foundation, not your home!

How can my story help you to manage your time more effectively?

To be successful in this highly competitive world you must learn how to work smarter than your colleagues, peers, and competition, but not harder.

Differentiate yourself by understanding how to prioritise your activities, avoid distractions and remain focused in a world of updates, notifications, instant messages and email.

In addition to knowing what will 'move the needle' and get results versus what's just busy work. We were born to live, not to spend our whole lives working and die with regrets!

This book is designed to help you recognise that you control your time and how you spend it. How efficiently you move through your to do list will depend on the decisions you make, the actions you take, the habits you create and your commitment to change.

"Efficiency is doing things right; effectiveness is doing the right things"
Peter Drucker

The better a time manager you become, the more you will notice your business, career and life will start to reflect these hopes, dreams, goals and aspirations. You'll also have more time to do what you love with the people you love. It is possible to create work/life balance!

One of the main factors that determines the success of an entrepreneur and a professional is their ability to confidently manage their time and be respected for having that skill. I genuinely believe that if you follow the advice and strategies I have provided within this book you will be able to do this. Not only that, you will have more time left over for you!

Clear patterns have emerged from the many events and courses I have attended, programs I have taken and from the business owners and professionals I have worked with - success leaves clues.

The successful have many traits in common, and although some are obvious, some are not.

Having spent many hours talking to and working with successful entrepreneurs and professionals, I have also spent time with those who struggle. There are common traits with their approach too, such as not prioritising their activities, spreading themselves too thinly, saying yes more often than no and becoming overwhelmed and anxious trying to get it all done.

I have a genuine passion to help ambitious entrepreneurs and professionals as well as those who struggle, to discover and achieve their full potential. Through my books and my coaching, mentoring, programs and training.

So let's get started and explore the methods and strategies that will enable you to turn your time into productivity.

Abigail Barnes

www.successbydesigntraining.com

TIME MANAGEMENT

HOW TO AVOID WASTING YOUR VALUABLE TIME

We all waste time every day, often without realising it. Examples are things like scrolling through social media and clicking on updates - looking at who's doing what and with whom...Which can take you off down all sorts of time consuming paths, phoning friends to discuss and dissect cryptic status updates, and or talking about the pictures they are tagged in (where was your invite?). A great activity if you want to lose an hour of your life every day. How is it helping you achieve your goals?

Reading articles/news online is another common distraction. While I encourage continuous learning, be wary of the time you spend going down internet 'research holes' clicking links, reading more, watching videos...and suddenly two hours have flown by and you've forgotten what you were supposed to be doing.

If there is a task that you must complete on a certain day focus, focus, focus and save your 'web-ducation' for a day and time you can dedicate to it. Even then, I would recommend that you set a physical (kitchen) timer to ensure that you limit the amount of time you spend doing this, as ten minutes can become two hours very quickly.

Emails are another common distraction. I teach the same strategy to my entrepreneur clients as I do to my professionals. We call it the Traffic Light Formula and it helps them prioritise their emails based on 3 criteria.

The other important thing to remember about emails is that they are often someone else's priority that they are trying to make yours. Most emails are requests or follow ups, and as you already have your to do list planned for the day, unless you are waiting for an important email and or your role is to respond to email requests then work out the best times of day to check them and then log out and focus on your to do list.

A useful tip is to set up rules in your inbox that automatically save certain email into specific folders (bypass your inbox) so that you can check them when you need to. This is your business/job and you have to remember that you are responsible for your time and are not a victim of it!

Watching the news to keep updated is a huge waste of time and not only that it can be a bit depressing and repetitive. That's not to say you shouldn't keep abreast of what is going on in the world, market, sector that you cover. I recommend you identify what sources of media are able to provide you with the information you need, set up alerts that consolidate it and organise a time that suits your schedule to catch up on it.

Consider creating positive and constructive diversions for those times when you need to take a mental break from work, such as looking at inspiring images on your vision board (more on this later), quotes from influential people, photos that make you smile. The best kind of distraction is laughter, so anything humorous is good.

The key to a successful, happy life is to take a holistic approach to your work/life balance. We use The 888 Formula as a framework to help our client's audit their life against 3 key metrics, Rest, Activities and Work (more on this later) and use it to identify where they are most out of balance.

Your mind needs nurturing just like your body. If you feed your body junk food, and don't exercise, then you are the one that pays the price for that decision. It is also your responsibility to find the right balance of lifestyle activities, hobbies and interests that bring you joy!

 TIME MANAGEMENT TIP 'Optimism is a daily choice that will save you time.' *Abigail Barnes*

If you read negative stories, watch depressing TV shows that focus on the lives of the most unhappy people, hang out with pessimists whose glass is always half-empty, then very soon your mind will believe that this is reality and you'll start to think and feel and act like they do.

However the reverse is also true. If you choose what you consume and decide only to read positive, inspirational, thought provoking things, watch shows that are uplifting and inspirational, and spend time with people who have overcome hardship or adversity and are doing what you want to do, then very quickly you will find that you are becoming the person, entrepreneur/professional that you want to be.

You control all of this – no one else. It is your job to constantly guard what goes into your mind, as whatever it experiences to be true it believes.

This is why there are so many 'versions of the truth'. People believe what is possible for them based on who they surround themselves with and what they consume. By making better decisions about what you focus on you will create new habits that will help you achieve your goals.

*"If you always do what you've always done,
you'll always get what you've always got."*
Henry Ford

It's commonly accepted that what you focus on, you will attract more of into your life, good and bad. Some people call this manifesting. On a very simple level your thoughts create your reality, the inspiration you get to take certain actions, but if you don't make the call, send the email, request to move the deadline then nothing will change in your physical reality.

There are very few things you can control in life, but what you allow yourself to think is something you can take control of.

It's not always easy, but it is possible. Whenever life has knocked me down, I have consciously decided to accept that it has happened for me, not to me. I run to my 'helicopter of possibility' to get perspective by looking at the bigger picture and see what I can learn from the experience. I could very easily have chosen the other approach on many occasions in my life, and I may have had good reason to feel sorry for myself – spinal surgery for scoliosis in my teens, numerous family deaths, multiple redundancies, and broken hearts. Each time I consciously made the decision to take control of my mind, and find something positive from each situation.

When life 'knocked me down' after my stroke it took me a long time to get back up again. My brain just couldn't seem to process the 'shock'. I had knocked at death's door, and been given a second chance. Overnight nothing meant anything anymore. Almost dying put everything into perspective, and the reality of how I'd been wasting my life and my time was overwhelming and isolating. Have you ever experienced something that changed your life over night and left you struggling to make sense of what happened and what your next step could be?

TIME MANAGEMENT TIP
*'When life knocks you down, don't say why me,
say ok life what next?'* **Abigail Barnes**

In the months after my stroke I filled my time and my mind with positivity bingeing on Tony Robbins, Les Brown, Zig Ziglar, Susan Jeffers, Robert Kiyosaki, T. Harv Eker, Wayne Dyer, Gabrielle Bernstein and Louise Hay.

I watched TED talks and YouTube videos, bought books and programs, studied the ways people became successful and achieved their goals and very soon my mind was alive with possibilities, and buzzing with ideas and gratitude for my second chance. Thank goodness for the Internet and technology that made all of this information so easy to access.

It would have been easy to slip into victim mode. I was only 32 when my stroke happened and my life changed over night. I refused to feel sorry for myself. Every day I would find something to be grateful for as soon as I woke up and still do. I walked away from the stroke with psychological not physical disabilities, that came with their own hidden consequences.

I live by a very simple mantra; if I don't like something I change it, because it's my life.

I am an optimist and choose to believe that my glass is always half-full, because I refuse to accept that it could be half-empty.

Each new day is an opportunity, a chance to make a difference no matter how big or small. If I can make a dog walker smile by saying 'good morning' while I am out on my daily walk, then I am being the change I want to see more of in this world!

GOOD ENOUGH

I used to tie myself in knots over this word, until one day I realised I get to decide what is enough because I report to me. If someone is not happy with something I do (within reason obviously, I must do what I said I will) I cannot control and am not responsible for how they feel. It is their expectations that need revising, not mine. As long as I work to the standards I set for myself, then whatever I do or deliver is good enough.

The concept of 'enough' is very closely linked to the feelings of expectation and guilt that we place on ourselves and others place on us. Time management, and recording how you spend your time (which is something we will look at later in the book) is an excellent way to help you recognise whether you are actually doing 'enough.' And if you are not, it can help you work out why not. This is important because once you have that awareness, change is inevitable.

It is through examining my own time management habits that I have been able to find true balance and happiness in my life. Believe me when I say I know that some of what I recommend in this book will be difficult. I have personally experienced that difficulty. But I assure you that once you take control of your time, you will find that you have more time than you ever thought possible. Your productivity and profitability will go through the roof, your friends and family will adjust and begin to accept and love the new improved you. You will also find that you become a 'change agent', and role model for those around you. Everyone admires people who take action and it's easier to learn from example!

*"Don't cheat us of your contribution,
give us what you have got"*
Steven Pressfield

It does take courage to change. But you are already courageous, which is why you invested in this book in the first place. You are hungry for that change too, and your curiosity drove you to discover how to create more time and turn that time into productivity and the life you want to be living!

THOUGHT PROVOCATEUR TIPS

- **Regulate your social media usage, recognise where it is and isn't adding value and take responsibility for it.**

- **Schedule in your internet research time and be militant about the amount of time you dedicate to it.**

- **Create an email strategy and start taking control of your inbox. Set up email rules so that you only have to deal with what is necessary, in the time that you allocate to reviewing them.**

- **Control your consumption of the news and TV, work on maintaining a positive frame of mind as this will lead to success.**

- **Consciously choose to be one of life's survivors, see things that happens to you as an opportunity to learn and get back in the game again!**

- **Make a commitment to read and watch motivational and educational content.**

- **Observe and change how you talk to yourself, choose to recognise progress and praise it!**

HOW TO USE YOUR TIME MORE EFFECTIVELY

The next section of the book is our five–step process, which will help you recognise how you are currently spending your time. It will help you to review your life and understand what the results say about you, and then present you with actions you can implement to regain control of your time, and provide some practical strategies to make your time more productive.

This is not a typical 'Time Management' book. It is not something that you are going to read and put on the shelf (otherwise known as shelf-development). The intention of this book is to open your eyes to the power that you have to become a confident time manager and to regain control your time, so that you can start living the life of your dreams.

It is possible, and all I require from you is an agreement with yourself that you won't put the book down when you don't feel like doing one of the activities I recommend. One thing I have learned again and again is that your biggest lessons and breakthroughs come at the times when you most want to quit!

You are responsible for everything in your business, and by the end of this book managing all of your roles and responsibilities will seem effortless. When it comes to your career, you will learn the power of controlling the controllables and still being the most productive person you know.

TIME MANAGEMENT TIP
'Either you control your time, or it will control you!'

Everything I recommend in this book and the programs we create for Success by Design Training has been trialed in my own life first. I resist accountability like the next person, but I make myself accountable for how I spend my time on a daily basis and focus on the tasks/activities where I add the most value (things only I can do) and outsource/delegate the rest.

To have a successful business/career it is important to identify what you are naturally good at and focus on it. This is what Sara Blakely (inventor of Spanx) did by bringing in a CEO to run her business, so she could focus on sales. I use a combination the of the CliftonStrengths Assessment, Human Design and Core Values Exercises with my Executive Coaching clients to help them identify their unique strengths and drivers, creating a solid foundation that they can build their happy balanced life on.

THOUGHT PROVOCATEUR TIPS

- Recognise that you are in control of what happens in your business/career because you are the boss of it!

- Be the visionary your business/organisation needs you to be, believe in yourself and trust that you know the right things to do, and if you don't then you can think of other people you can ask because you are a problem solver!

5 STEP PROCESS FOR TURNING YOUR TIME INTO PRODUCTIVITY

STEP 1 – TRACK YOUR TIME

To have a clear understanding of how you are currently spending your time I want you to track your time for a week. This record is for your eyes only.

Be honest about what you record. After all, you are doing this for yourself, so there is no point in making it up. Visit our website and download a copy of the timesheet. I recommend that you print it off and handwrite it, so that when we come to reviewing it in the next section, a hard copy showing how you are currently spending your time will have more impact.

Timesheet - Audit your week

	Monday	Tuesday	Wednesday	Thurday	Friday	Saturday	Sunday
AM							
PM							

TIP - Visit www.successbydesigntraining.com to download a hard copy of the timesheet document.

Do not be tempted to do this task for a couple of days and then start making changes, trying to fix the problems for yourself. These are habits that you are likely to have had for a long time, so they are not going to be that easy to change. I know because I tried this short cut myself, and it didn't work, for some of the reasons I will outline below.

TIME MANAGEMENT TIP
*'It is not who you are that will stop you,
it is who you think you are!'*

Some of your current habits affect other people, and if you suddenly change overnight you are going to come up against resistance from them. Which will cause you to question the need to change, and the book risks becoming 'shelf development' - and we don't want that because we want you to become the confident time manager you deserve to be.

Recording and reviewing is the best way to learn and to change habits. It is common sense, but it's so easy to become absorbed in the day to day running of your business/doing your job that you forget what you know – you are so busy chipping away at what's in front of you, that you are unable to see the bigger picture.

Sometimes we all need something or someone to come along and give us a reality check, and that is the purpose of this exercise. I am that person not because I know more than you, but because I can objectively say STOP for a minute, take a step back and let's review what you are doing and why. Track your week (including the weekend) so we have something to review in the next section. Start tomorrow (whatever day that is, and track your time for 7 days).

We are all a product of our upbringing and education – both life and academic. The key to success is to never stop learning, never to assume that you know it all, and to periodically pause, assess, learn, and then adapt what you do to incorporate the new knowledge that you have accrued. Mastering the skill of reflection is the difference between a business/professional that will excel and one that will fail.

Document a seven-day week as this will allow you to review how you are currently spending your leisure time as well as work time.

Include everything from the moment that you wake up to the time you go to bed, as there are answers to be found from all of it. They say that success leaves a clue; well I believe that the same is true in reverse. Record your exercise, social media scrolling, phone calls, time spent with family, friends and your partner, cooking, eating, socialising, TV consumption and sleeping.

Be as specific as you can because the information will make it easier for you to spot patterns that way. And as I said earlier be honest. This exercise is for your benefit.

No one else needs to see it, and if you cheat you are only lying to yourself.

To make a change you need to identify where you are now, and then decide where you want to be. The change equals the steps that you need to take in order to get there. Remember that if you are building a new property it needs a solid foundation. Being an entrepreneur/ambitious professional you are likely to be a high achiever. If we rush this part of the building process you will end up with the Leaning Tower of Pisa – I'm sure that's not how you envision things going!

THOUGHT PROVOCATEUR TIPS

- **Commit to tracking how you currently spend your time for 7 days.**

- **Control your desire to start fixing things until you have read more of the book and learnt more techniques for time management.**

- **Be honest and non judgmental in how you approach this exercise the results are for your eyes only!**

CASE STUDY - Suzanne Shaw (Singer, Actress, Entrepreneur)
www.thehappyhealthclub.com

Describe a typical working day.

Prior to the pandemic I would have been on the road, in face-to-face meetings, interviews, photoshoots, rehearsals, or performing.

This is my typical working day (in lockdown 2020/21 VERY different from my previous working days before the pandemic).

- *Wake up 6.30am and start my day with a coffee. If I'm not combining my workout with my online wellness community The Happy Health Club then I workout or run between 7-8am.*

- *8-8.30am I get ready and 8.35am is the school drop off (if open)*

- *9am I try to journal before starting my day! Normally I put together a 30 min slot to write my ideas and goals.*

- *9.30-13.00 emails, social media content, zoom meetings and a bit of time on Clubhouse (in a Club I run or co moderate).*

- *13.00 If I'm able to set time aside for lunch I will take time away from my desk and have lunch, sometims even in a park, or get out for a walk to clear my head space.*

- *14.00-15.30 more calls, Zooms or content planning*

- *15.30/16.00-19.00 I set this time aside for family: cooking eating dinner and the childrens bed time.*

- *19.00-21.00 either social media for work, or watch, listen or read something I can learn from.*

- *21.00-21.15 write my to do list for the following day!*

- *21.30 I will try my best to be in bed so I get a decent nights sleep zzz.*

Are there any times of the day that you are more productive, and if so, why do you think that's the case?

Mornings always! Particularly after a run. Running really helps my creativity and is a great problem solver! Since taking up running I've become much more productive.

What distracts you from work and how do you maintain focus?

Social media can open up a rabbit hole and before you know it you have spent precious time exploring the world of the Kardashians, without even being a fan!! I literally have to tell myself "Off" out loud!

What change/s have you made to increase your productivity?

My lifestyle! Quitting drinking has been the making of my productivity! 90% of the time I do what I say I'm going to do, and that has helped my confidence no end! It has helped so many areas of my life... I eat better, so therefore I am in a better mood most of the time, I sleep better, therefore I am in a better mood most of the time, I exercise more... you know where I'm going with this!! Yes better mood and that translates into productivity!

What tips would you give someone who wants to improve how they spend their time?

Practice mindfulness - it is best practiced through journaling.

Some examples of things you can write down:
- what triggers you
- what distracts you
- how you feel after a meal
- what foods help with your energy levels
- track your productivity on the days you exercise versus not
- how much sleep you get & how you feel

This information you learn from journaling will help you understand yourself better as well as how to get the most out of your time each day and create your own tailored time plan.

STEP 2 – ANALYSE YOUR RESULTS

You have kept your hard copy timesheet for seven days now. That means we should have some meaningful and honest (hopefully) data to analyse. If you haven't done it STOP reading now and complete Step 1.

It is at this stage that we start to spot patterns. You might not have had a 'normal' week but that doesn't matter, life is what it is and the time management techniques I will be sharing with you in this book are applicable to whatever kind of a week you have had.

If this does concern you, wait until you have captured a 'normal' week before you move forward, but beware of procrastination sabotage, there is no normal week!

"All I ever knew is that I never wanted to be average"
Michael Jordan

Key points to note are the time that you got up in the morning and went to bed, because these will dictate firstly how much time you are giving yourself each day, to complete your activities and secondly how much energy you have to do them.

If you get up around 05.30/06.30 each day for example then you can get tasks done before the rest of the world is really up and about. If you go to bed any later than 10pm and you are tired the next day, ask yourself honestly if the late night was worth it? If it was then don't beat yourself up, that's life (sometime you will have to work to whatever time is necessary to get the job done), but if it wasn't make smarter choices next time around. This is not a lecture it is simply me pointing out that you control how you feel, not someone else.

To live the life that you dream of, you will need to take control of how you spend your time!

If you have children who are waking up during the night then this will affect your sleep but it won't last forever. You may need to work out ways to adapt to this, and hacks to help you catch up on sleep like napping for 20 minutes when you can (more on the power of napping later).

Did you spend any time on self care? We teach all our clients something called the 8-Minute Secret.

How to create a simple daily self care routine made up of 8-minute activities that fall under 3 pillars. Movement, Mindset and Meditation.

You can't give from an empty cup, it's important to spend time throughout the day doing activities that replenish your energy levels and keep you motivated.

How were you spending your time when you were working? What patterns can you notice, who or what were your biggest distractions (emails, phone, instant messenger apps)? According to research it takes around 20 minutes to focus, and 20 minutes to refocus when we get distracted.

It is important to identify your strengths and weaknesses. When was your most productive time of the day for example, and when was your least productive time?

Once you have this information there are two techniques we teach our clients one is called the DLD Formula (Daily Lock Down) and the other is a concept known as task/activity chunking.

Social Media – how much time did you spend on it, both personal and business/career related. How determined are you to grow your profile online? Now dispassionately review how much value you are getting from the time you spent on Instagram, Facebook, Twitter, LinkedIn in terms of enquiries/leads/connections. If social media does genuinely make a contribution to your business/career then make some time to research tools that can help you automate/schedule things.

TIP - Visit our **website** for more tips, tools and training.

Where your social media usage is personal versus business/career related, use it consciously to avoid wasting large amounts of time mindlessly scrolling.

Review your time tracking worksheet and be honest with yourself, decide whether the social media you are consuming is enhancing your life and aligns with your desire to be more productive. If it does, diarise the times you will spend on certain apps and set time limits for them.

If it doesn't add to your life, cut it out.

Until you become a master at time management setting a physical (kitchen) timer can also help you keep track of the time you are actually spending on social media. At this stage I want to encourage you to do some research into the addictive nature of the platforms. They have been designed to keep you coming back for more.

Care Bear – How much time did you spend caring for other people in the last seven days? Family, friends, neighbours, strangers?

Review your time and look for patterns. Are there people you might be doing too much for? Is it time to a step back from some family/ friendship/ employee/colleague relationships?

Are there people who need to learn how to fish as opposed to you providing the fish for them? Are there people in your life that you are drowning in fish who would benefit from you teaching them how to fish for themselves?

Now might be a good time for you to honestly and lovingly review some habits, patterns and routines. This doesn't mean that you no longer care, it means that you care so much that you are able to recognise that doing everything for everyone doesn't actually help anyone in the long run. It ends up leaving you with less time and energy to focus on your business, career or life.

We are born with the answers to all our questions, however we get into the habit of looking outside of ourselves for them. We become reliant on others to supply them.

By practicing loving detachment you will encourage self–reliance and find that you automatically get more time back to do with as you wish. If it has always been your job to fix problems and resolve situations, then it is important to recognise that the best way for you to do this is to let people work out the answers for themselves (obviously this doesn't apply to hazardous situations, use your common sense) and trust that the more you allow them to do things for themselves the better they will become at it.

It may seem that they no longer 'need' you, but what you will find is that the relationship you now share will be stronger and better as a result of the trust you are placing in them to resolve their own challenges, and the trust they begin to have in themselves to be able to handle things that previously they allowed others to do for them. Now they can fish, and you can do whatever you want to with the time that you have reclaimed!

THOUGHT PROVOCATEUR TIPS

- **Begin by looking for obvious patterns.**

- **Remember not to judge yourself based on what you discover from doing this exercise, no one is perfect, and identification is the first step to bringing about successful change.**

STEP 3 – WHAT YOUR RESULTS SAY ABOUT YOU

We have touched on a few topics so far, in this section I'll introduce you to our six time-wasting archetypes in more detail (say hello to cartoon Abigail).

Below is a table summarising their characteristics along with a solution.

Characteristic	Solution
Social media Junkie	Discipline
Chatter Box	Organisation
Care-Bear	Resolution
Jack of all trades	Outsource/Delegate
Procrastination	Routine/structure
Travel-Bunny	Planning

SOCIAL MEDIA JUNKIE

We touched on this in the previous section, but the main way that you can control this part of your personality initially is through discipline (until it becomes a habit). Social media is life, it's where we connect, converse and keep updated, but the key is to work out how to control it, and not let it control you.

For an entrepreneur how you use social media will be different to a professional's use of it. But both users want to improve their visibility online, and you can do this without spending 24/7 posting, replying and liking. Contrary to popular belief social media is not a popularity contest, all it takes is consistency, and a plan that's tailored to your goal and audience.

The first practical tip is to understand the goal of social media in your business/profession and then look for ways you can you can repurpose your content across multiple platforms. Below is a list of the places that you are likely to need to create/keep updated on a daily, weekly, monthly basis. Start by creating the content for your website and then look for ways to edit this for use across other digital channels.

(The last part may be more relevant to my entrepreneurs, and side hustlers)

Website		Linkedin Profile/Business Page
Blog		Instagram Account
Facebook Profile/Business Page		YouTube Channel
Google My Business Account		Email strategy
Twitter Account		

TIP – Visit our **website** for more tips, tools and training.

Your audience is not going to have time to keep up to date with your message on all of the above channels at once, so it is not going to harm your business if you repurpose your own content. Actually if you manage to do it correctly it should just look like you are delivering a consistent message across all media. There is no point in reinventing the wheel in business, it exists already, just work out how you can make it roll better!

I suggested discipline as the key word for your approach to social media. Once you have your plan you have an approach, but you still need to make sure that you keep to this plan and stick to the time that you are now allocating. Until you have mastered this new approach set a timer to ensure that you don't over run, as it's so easy to get lost in an online rabbit hole for hours! Use your mobile phone alarm or a kitchen timer and set app limits. When the time is up, wherever you are make a note of it and come back to what you were doing later. Don't be tempted to carry on, as you will never finish what you were supposed to be doing.

At this stage it is also important to look back over the time that you have spent and to honestly identify things that you didn't need to do, and look at how they affected your ability to complete the activities that you had set yourself. The reason that I advise you to stop and come back to what you were doing later is that by doing this you are taking charge of your mind, saying 'no', and stopping it from being undisciplined.

It may sound draconian, but this is your business/career, and if you want to become more productive then you have to take control! Try disciplining yourself in the third person; review progress as though you were reviewing someone else's actions. Ask yourself, if a member of staff/colleague had acted as you have just acted, would you be pleased? If the answer is no, then learn from the situation - you are in charge of performance!

While you are trialing this new way of working, observe how over time you become much more efficient and effective, and recognise that you are beginning to learn just how long a task should actually take.

CHATTERBOX

Humans are social creatures and we like to interact with others. There is nothing wrong with this, but it is important to note where the need for social interaction, business conversations and general chitchat meet. Prioritise any calls that you need to make, have a clear outcome for each one and dedicate a set amount of time to them. It is best to allocate a block of time to make all your calls, as you will start to build up a good rhythm, especially if you have to make sales calls, chunking will increase your productivity.

If you want to manage your time more effectively and are dedicated to creating a better work life balance, then now is the time to take the control back and cut out the chitchat. Is it really help-ing your business/career/productivity to know that your friend's neighbour just mowed their lawn in their boxers, and not just any old boxers, a pair of cartoon boxers. Engaging in these kinds of conversations on a regular basis does not help you to complete your to-do list any quicker. They also become a habit, something that your mind starts to crave as a way of distracting you from the task at hand (our minds are crafty resistant things that prefer gossip and procrastination over work).

Therefore get organised, make the calls that you need to make, be as polite and conversational as the call requires you to be (be normal) but at all costs avoid daily gossip calls which before you realise it have become a habit for you and the caller, stealing your time, focus and productivity, and harming your chances of creating the life of your dreams!

You only get one life, I strongly suggest that you focus on living it, and that you don't waste your time and energy discussing the lives of others. Choose to focus on activities that enhance your life and wellbeing not de-tract from it!

CARE-BEAR

We touched on this characteristic in the previous section. Having invested in this book I'm willing to guess that people see you as a problem solver, you are the person everyone comes to for advice on how to resolve situations in their lives. You are good at fixing problems, almost too good, so much so it is likely that you are always being asked to 'help'.

Let's take a step back from this and look at it for what it really is. Consciously or subconsciously you have created a situation where you are needed, which in turn makes you feel wanted and loved. What if I were to tell you that you are already wanted and loved, but that the situation you have created is actually harming you and those around you? Because your focus needs to be on finding ways to be more productive so that you can spend quality time with the people you care about.

By always providing solutions for others, and even on occasions actually executing your own plan, you are stopping them from gaining independence and learning and growing from their own life journey. Without recognising this situation for what it really is, because you think it is about 'helping' you are actually spending a lot of time resolving short-term issues which in turn lead to longer-term problems and co-dependency.

Don't misunderstand me, I'm not telling you to stop helping those in genuine need of support. I'm inviting you to recognise that the next time there is a problem that needs your help that you take a moment and ask yourself this question. If I provide the solution here am I really helping the person learn the lessons that they need to learn? If the answer is no then it's time for you to start teaching people how to tap into the answers that they have inside themselves.

TIME MANAGEMENT TIP
'Be an effective time management leader, those around will learn from your example'

By helping others what you're doing is not wrong, but sometimes the best way to help is to be more of a coach, to allow them to come to their own conclusions, versus solving their problems for them. Ask them a question like what do you think you should do? to help them become more self-confident, self-reliant and resilient.

TIP - For quick tips about coaching please visit our <u>website.</u>

Once you learn to recognise when you are genuinely needed to provide the answers, and when you are not, you will recover a lot of wasted time from your day, and feel less obligated to solve everyone's 'problems'.

JACK OF ALL TRADES

In business and work you are always going to be juggling a number of roles. It's great to be resourceful, but it's also important not to get side tracked from what you're focusing on.

It's important to understand from the outset what 'return' you expect for the time you are investing into the activity at hand. Put another way, is what you are doing right now going to have the greatest impact on achieving your goal/s, progressing a project, 'doing your job', growing your business?

If the answer is no, then the question needs to be who else could do it and or perhaps should be doing it?

There are many activities that can keep an entrepreneur and a professional busy all day. Keeping busy is not the name of the game, being productive is, doing the right activities at the right time, and understanding how to say no without saying no, which is one of our most popular trainings.

For my business owner readers, recruiting staff can take time and resources, but there are other options in the form of outsourcing. With the advent of the Internet it has never been easier; there is a hugely talented global workforce out there ready and waiting to work for you. The options are endless, you can find people to work with you for a one off task, a project, for a certain number of hours per week/month as well as full-time support. As your Business needs change, your recruiting strategy can too.

Below is a short list of some of the business activities that you can out-source:

Website creation (SEO)	Competitor/Market Research
Copy writing	Social Media Management
Customer Service Team (virtual, manage calls & email)	Email Campaigns (create funnels)
Assistant/VA (calendar, email, travel plans)	Fulfillment (posting your products)

There really is no limit to the things that you can outsource in your business, all you need is vision, organisation, patience and the ability to communicate your proposition to others. Later in the book I go into greater detail about some ways to outsource more successfully. This way of working will free up so much more time for you to focus on more productive activities that will grow your business and your revenue.

This way of working will help you get access to global talent at accessible rates that can do the work while you sleep due to the difference in timezones. Remember this is a form of delegation not abdication. It is still your responsibility to manage them and the process, nothing just works. The results will be as good as your brief and style of management.

To state the obvious don't try out a new member of your virtual team on your biggest project where timings and budgets are critical. You need to build trust with your virtual staff just as you would with physical staff. While 99% of the time your interactions will be seamless there will always be the 1% of the time when things don't go to plan, so don't outsource and then totally take your hands off the wheel, this is still your business, you are still in charge, and the buck still stops with you. I will cover more on outsourcing later in the book.

For my professional readers, I hope that this conversation has given you some food for thought. What activities on your to do list could be delegated to someone else within your organisation, and or require a new member of staff to manage them? As with all things in life there may not be the resource, budget or opportunity to do something today...but this exercise will help you to identify what's stopping you from being more productive, and or what you need to do first on a daily basis. There is no perfect organisation, or work day, there is information that helps you have a better understanding of your performance against the KPI's you are measured against, and to keep a record of it.

PROCRASTINATION

Procrastination, or resistance is a form of self-sabotage. It is the voice that entices you to go online, make a phone call, get up from your desk and make a drink "you've been working really hard it says - of course you deserve a break", but if you look at the precise time that the voice began to tempt you, it's usually right before you're about to do something that either you are unsure about, or it's a new task/activity that requires more thought.

From a scientific point of view, the brain is hardwired to do this. It categorises the new activity as a possible threat, and sends a signal to protect itself until it has had time to review and understand the risk level associated with the activity.

TIME MANAGEMENT TIP
'FEAR is a four letter word…if you are going to let that stop you, then what else will stop you achieving the business success that you strive for?'

The brain's job is to keep you safe, to keep you alive. It loves to be in the comfort zone, doing the same things over and over again. It's really helpful too, it creates unconscious programs that run automatically to help you to not have to think too hard. That way you will live to see another day and it won't have to worry about running out of energy. Your brain uses around 20% of your daily food intake as fuel and new activities use more.

If you try something new who knows what could happen, so it distracts you. You begin bartering with yourself, saying things like 'if I do XYZ fun stuff now then after that I will sit down and get on with what I need to do'. You tell yourself that the problem isn't one of trying to avoid the task, it is just that you need to work up to it, get into the right frame of mind, do X first instead. Sound familiar? The trouble with this approach is that X soon becomes Y, which then becomes Z… oh and then it's too late to do the task but that's ok 'I will do it tomorrow'. Those immortal words!

Tomorrow comes around and your procrastinating, resistant mind is still frantically working overtime to create more ways to put off the task again. The brain is running an interference pattern, because who knows what will happen once you do the thing you have never done before!

Here is where you need to break this pattern once and for all. Structure and organisation are called for, and with practice and patience they will become new habits. The longer you have available to think about something that you don't really want to do, the more time you have to create 701 reasons why you shouldn't do it today. By structuring your activities so that one thing links into another, you give yourself no time to generate resistance, you trick your mind with momentum!

Remember - this is your business/career. Success and failure are in your hands, it's your decision. The ultimate loser in all of this will be you and the people you love.

Why do you want to become more productive?

This book will help you become a more confident time manager with the lifestyle to match, but only if you take action!

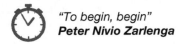

"To begin, begin"
Peter Nivio Zarlenga

By continuing to procrastinate it is you that is sabotaging your dreams!

I love this quote, it short circuits my own resistance and procrastination instantly, because it leaves my mind with nothing else to do but BEGIN! It is concise and to the point and I urge you to make a note of it and keep it handy for times of procrastination; say to yourself – just begin!

My other tip is to thank your brain for the job it's doing to keep you safe, to assure it that 'you've got this and will handle whatever comes up from doing something new'.

Gone are the days of motivating and forcing our way through things - think of your brain like a computer that needs a software update and you are the only one that can do the update, by taking new actions.

Coming back to some science again, when you do this you are effectively rewiring circuits in your brain and creating new neural pathways, a field of research known as neuroplasticity. This is something I am fascinated by and have spent many hours studying to better understand how my brain has rewired itself after my stroke (brain injury).

CASE STUDY - Dr Lynda Shaw (Neuroscientist, Author, Speaker)
www.drlyndashaw.com

Describe a typical working day

I awake at about 7am and go to the gym (well not during lockdown) or do some kind of exercise. I'm usually at my desk between 9 and 9.30.

My day is full of research, writing, communicating with clients, social media, marketing and delivery. What I mean by delivery is keynote speaking, workshops, corporate programmes or running my online programmes. This can be virtual or face to face.

Some of my meetings are via old fashioned phone and that is when I walk and talk. It's delightful how many people I talk to on the phone decide to walk too. It's a great way to conduct meetings whilst getting some fresh air and respite from screens.

I normally finish work around 6pm, but some evenings zoom calls continue until about 8pm. This is clearly a long day, but each day is different and sometimes personal tasks break things up as well.

Are there any times of the day that you are more effective, and if so, why do you think that's the case?

I'm most creative when I first wake up, when I'm in that half asleep state. I don't bother creating anything in the evenings, I guarantee I will erase it all the next day. I've learnt to wait until next morning when the creative ideas have had a chance to develop as I sleep.

What distracts you from work and how do you maintain focus?

Maintaining focus can be quite challenging, especially when there is much to focus on. When this happens I set myself little targets to reach in 45 mins or whatever is appropriate for the job. Then I get up and move around, maybe take a 10 minute walk and allow my thoughts to brew before my next 45 minute chunk.

What change/s have you made to increase your productivity?

My topic is very complicated, and I pride myself on my ability to simplify information without making it simplistic.

Each time I succeed in increasing my productivity I have noticed that it is because I have changed the way I think or do something and it often involves simplifying the task. Sometimes we overthink or over complicate things and that can hinder our progress.

What tips would you give someone that wants to improve how they spend their time?

Work out why you're doing something. Will it increase productivity Will it lead directly to meetings you need or want? Will it help some- one else? Will it be fun?

If you're spending your very precious time doing something that is not going to tick one or more of these boxes, then perhaps it's not worth doing. Even if it's just a tiny step, as long as it's in the right direction then it's worth it. If not, don't do it. Be honest with yourself.

TRAVEL BUNNY

How you choose to spend your time is your decision, you are the boss of your life. There will be times as an entrepreneur and professional when you will need to do things face-to-face, and travel to meetings/the office as well as times you can work remotely/from home. If you can choose when you travel be mindful of what different times mean for the rest of your life (during the work day, versus early mornings, evenings, or weekends).

How you allocate your 24-hour day is creating the business/career lifestyle that you have. This time stealing archetype is a reminder that work travel, and even commuting uses up your finite time on a daily basis, something we will cover more later in the book when we talk about The 888 Formula.

By planning your week and your time it will become much easier to make your 24 hours days more productive. Ask yourself a question like how can I maximise my time today? Ask it daily. If you are going into the office/to a meeting how can you spend that time/commute? What work could you do and or what personal admin can you catch up on? As long as you are meeting your deadlines, organisations are much more relaxed/flexible about how you actually do the work, versus when you do it, and if it's your own business...you have the final say!

Laptops are lighter and mobile phones and tablets enable us to do many of the activities that had us desk bound in the past. Once you begin planning your time you will get good at making the most of every moment, even wifi is less of a problem these days as you can tether your mobile phones and use that data if needed. Cloud based software means you can access and work on documents across devices.

It really has never been easier to turn your time into productivity.

What we covered in this section of the book is the tip of the Time Management iceberg. I hope that learning more about our six 'time-wasting' archetypes has helped you to spot some of the patterns that came up for you during your time tracking. Now you have a clearer understanding about where they might have come from, a have some strategies you can start to create new habits. You will find more information on our website, along with the books we recommend to support your on-going education.

TIP – Visit our <u>website</u> for more tips, tools and training.

One word of caution. Beware of your resistance or procrastination voice; now that it knows you are on to it, it could send you on a huge mission to 'discover yourself' which is code for reading a load more books so that you don't have to make any immediate changes. Hopefully the way I have worded this book and the investment that you have made in purchasing and reading this far, means that you do not fall into that trap! By all means continue your education. I encourage it. But don't do it at the expense of immediate change and progress as a result of this book now.

Results come from actions, not more knowledge!

THOUGHT PROVOCATEUR TIPS

- **Recognise and own up to the habits which are apparent in your own results, your time management challenges.**

- **Use the archetypes to help you understand the reasons why you have been managing your time how you have until now.**

- **Consider applying the solutions suggested in this section to address your time management challenges.**

- **Be vigilant for procrastination and all its manipulative ways.**

STEP 4 – TIME TO TAKE ACTION (OUR AGREEMENT)

This is the section of the book where it's time to start doing something with the information you are learning. – Talking about things is the easy part, but your results will only follow the actions you take.

So sit up in your chair, bed, or wherever you are reading this book, and place your hand on your heart. Close your eyes and take two deep cleansing breaths, breathing in through your nose and out through your mouth.

Open your eyes and read the agreement you are going to make with yourself, either out loud or in your head (it is up to you).

Personally I like to read things first in my head, then I re-read them out loud (but that's me) - do whatever works for you!

TIP – Visit our website www.successbydesigntraining.com download a hard copy of this agreement, sign it, date it, and keep it close to hand.

My Agreement:

I ....(name) recognise and acknowledge there are things I am currently doing, that are stealing my time.

I commit to making the changes necessary to have more time, so I can have the balanced lifestyle I want.

I agree to recognise when I fall back into my old destructive habits, and to revisit the parts of this book that are relevant to helping me be responsible for, and not a victim of, my time.

I understand that there will be times when change may seem hard and painful, but I believe in my courage to follow through on my actions and that the lifestyle I can have will be worth it.

I vow to never use time as an excuse again because I understand that I control how I spend my time and that it is my sole responsibility to change and take charge.

I ....(name) sign my agreement to this commitment with myself,

Date ....

STEP 5 – TURNING TIME INTO PRODUCTIVITY

Now that we have identified how you are currently spending your time, reviewed what this means for your business/career/life and you have agreed to take action.

The following section gives you five strategies you can try out in your work and life (where relevant).

Some strategies for turning your time into productivity are listed below. This chapter will give you a high level introduction to each one and suggest ways you could use it (if it's not relevant to you right now, skip this section, and if you're intrigued, do some more research).

Outsourcing/Delegation	Events/Workshops
Training (Student for life)	Coaches & Mentors
Networking	

OUTSOURCING:

As a business owner outsourcing gives you back the time to focus on what you do best, and gives you more time for client facing work, while still being able to scale and grow your business.

By building relationships with your outsourcers that are based on trust and respect you will be able to create a (global) team with which you can accomplish just about anything.

Outsourcing provides you with access to global talent. The ability to increase your 'team' without the hassle of full time recruitment (interviews), and payroll admin that for a small/lifestyle or lean enterprise will prove to be invaluable for lower stress business growth.

Just because you can do it, doesn't mean you should keep doing it.

Outsourcing allows you to move from working 'in your business', where you are responsible for everything, to working 'on your business', where effectively you step into more of a project manager role, outsourcing activities to freelance experts that you manage. Responding to their questions, providing clarification via email or project management systems, giving guidance and support. Giving you more time to spend on revenue generating activities that will grow your business.

You are the expert in what you do, and outsources are the experts in what they do. Resolve any needs you may have to be in control of everything, trust issues, and fears, and embrace a new way of working.

TIME MANAGEMENT TIP
*'Change your mindset, and you
will change your results!'*

The list of activities you can outsource is endless and only limited by your imagination, below is a list of activities to get you started:

- **Website Creation**
  - SEO
  - Social media strategy

- **Copy Writing**
  - Web content
  - Blogs (for Facebook, Linkedin, Website)
  - Sales copy for email marketing

- **Customer Service**
  - Email support
  - Call center
  - Virtual team

- **Personal Assistant**
  - Manage your diary
  - Book travel/accommodation
  - Deal with basic emails

- **Market Research**
  - Industry/Sector

- Product
- Competitor

- **Social media**
  - Basic profile
  - Maintain basic presence
  - Facebook/Linkedin/Google my Business /Pinterest/Instagram/Twitter/Youtube account management

- **Email campaigns**
  - Create emails
  - Manage email strategy (timings)
  - Provide reporting

- **Fulfillment**
  - Manage physical stock
  - Manage distribution

- **Accountancy**
  - VAT returns
  - Book keeping
  - Accounts (P&L)

7 REASONS TO OUTSOURCE:

1. There is a massive pool of talent in the world today
2. You can literally outsource everything
3. Outsourcing allows you to concentrate on what you are good at, your core competencies
4. You don't ever have to speak to, or meet with them if you don't want to
5. Outsourcing can be very cost effective
6. The cost of living in many countries outside of the UK or US is far lower, therefore the cost of outsourcing is a lot cheaper (you are putting them in the top 10% of earners in their own country, you are giving them a chance to have a 'skilled' job and provide for their families)
7. Outsourcers can work while you sleep due to the time differences

DELEGATION

As an employee, outsourcing would be known as delegation, and it could range from working with external people such as suppliers, agencies, event/travel/training companies, as well as internal teams and departments within your organisation.

During my corporate career I was responsible for the relationships management of a huge number of different suppliers each of which provided the expertise we needed to complete a project, hit a KPI, deliver an event, communicate with clients or advertise/promote their investment funds/managers/services.

They saved me time and the organisation money by not having to work out how to do what they either had the connections, relationships, skills, experience or expertise to do for us.

What is there on your to do list right now that is stopping you from being more productive, and doing the job you were employed to do?

While I appreciate it may not be possible for you to delegate those activities to anyone today. By identifying what is slowing you down, holding you back, stopping you from being more efficient and effective on a day-to-day basis, you will have the information you need to make a case for more headcount, or internal support to delegate tasks/activities to other people or departments when the time comes. You will also be able to use it at appraisal, bonus, and promotion time to highlight your contribution.

7 REASONS TO DELEGATE:

1. Sometimes you are not the best person to do the activity

2. You will empower your team/colleagues by using their skills

3. Delegation gives you more time for the activities your organisation needs your expertise for

4. Someone else is an expert and can do the job in half the time it would take you to do it

5. Delegation can be more cost effective for your organisation

6. You can be more strategic, and work on the tasks that move the needle

7. It can help reduce overwhelm and burnout

TRAINING

According to the most recent scientific research humans are born with some 'basic programming' such as the need to survive (avoiding dangerous things, until classified as safe), the desire to reproduce and most interestingly the motivation to communicate with others (be that with words, cave paintings or sign language).

Which means that everything else is learned behaviour. Things that we picked up throughout our life from:

1. Caregivers (Parents)
2. Teachers
3. Religious Organisations
4. Culture/Media
5. Country/Politics

STUDENT FOR LIFE

In recent years scientists have discovered that the human brain continues to rewire itself throughout its lifetime (neuroplasticity). The past does not have to dictate the future, knowledge is power, because it gives you proof of what's possible and if you take action and use what you know/learn then things can change!

"Entrepreneurship is a process, not a job or a profession"
Robert Kiyosaki

As an entrepreneur/professional you will never know everything, it is your job to understand who to call when you need help, and to take responsibility for your own continuous professional development (CPD).

This education can take the form of the books you read, podcasts you listen to, talks you watch, courses you take, programs you invest in and events you attend (whether business related or not), because as I have mentioned a number of times already, success leaves clues.

I am a member of lots of different groups that not only provide me with current and timely information, but also allow me to spend time with people who are doing what I am doing, or aspire to do. You become like the people you spend the most time with, so spend as much time as you can around successful, motivated people that inspire and uplift you.

"To be nobody but yourself in a world which is doing its best day and night to make you like everybody else means to fight the hardest battle which any human being can fight and never stop fighting."
E.E. Cummings

Become an information machine, use the success stories of entrepreneurs, professionals, experts, peers and people you admire as proof of what's possible, surround yourself with positivity and proof all day long.

Commit to remaining teachable and open to learning new things, with a growth mindset versus fixed mindset as Carol Dweck calls it (check her out).

We were born to live, to love, to grow and to evolve which is something we can't do if we don't question what we believe and try new things. What's worse, to know you don't like something or to spend your life wondering? We come here once...try things (within reason obviously).

Find and watch inspiring interviews on YouTube, as well as TED/TEDx talks and documentaries about things and people you are interested in. Try out their suggestions, habits and strategies because if it worked for them it could work for you too, and if it doesn't keep experimenting. Beware of Internet rabbit holes (set a timer).

NETWORKING

Life is not only about what you know, but also about who you know. How many times have you heard that? Do not underestimate the power of your network, you never know when a conversation about one thing may lead to another. People tend to fall into two types:

1. What can I get from you: people who ask their list of ten standard, questions, and if nothing of interest comes up they move on.

2. What can I do for you: people who understand that in order to get anything in life, they first have to give, or at least build a relationship with you. The more you are willing to give in life the more you are likely to receive - it's called the law of reciprocity.

"We make a living by what we get. We make a life by what we give."
Winston Churchill

If you are a giver then you are likely to receive, but you have to accept you won't know when things will come, or who they might come from. Giving and receiving has to be a way of life, and not tied to expectations. For this to happen you will have to adopt a way of living in which you are 'constantly networking'. Where every conversation that you have with someone becomes an exchange full of possibilities, on the basis that no one ever knows when or where the next connection may appear.

Networking is an exchange of information, approach it from the angle of what could you learn from this new person and what can you do for them, not what can they do for you. Develop active listening skills, practice being present and become genuinely interested in what others have to say. Smile, ask questions and people will remember you because you listened to what they had to say.

Successful people understand the value of a good network, they recognise that they don't need to have all the answers in every situation because the power lies in having access to a network of people who do.

EVENTS

Keep up to speed with what is going on in your industry and sector. Just as in the previous section I highlighted the importance of networking, I also recommend that each year you make a note of when the key events for your industry are, and that you sign up for them and book them into your diary at the start of the year/when they come up.

TIME MANAGEMENT TIP
Invest time in building a global network of peers and experts.

By attending events you will not only be able to keep up to speed with what is going on in your industry, but you will also be able to network with like-minded peers.

People I have met at events have become my coaches, teachers, clients, guests on my podcast, friends, and in some cases have been instrumental in me totally changing the path of my life and career. The events also helped me to address things like my relationship with money, approach to business, limiting beliefs and imposter syndrome.

COACHES & MENTORS

In this section I will address three questions I get asked a lot:

1. What is a coach?
2. What is a mentor?
3. Do I have to pay for them?

TIME MANAGEMENT TIP
'Spend time with people who are good time managers, their strategies will influence you and strengthen yours'

1. What is a coach? Depending on who you ask you will get a variety of different answers, and since this is my book I'll give you mine.

A coach is someone trained to ask you, the client, questions about the goal/s you want to achieve, help you identify your blocks, find your motivation, agree what you will do, by when and hold you accountable.

They do not need to know anything about your business/sector/life their job is to coach you to identify the actions you will take, and to support you (with accountability) for however long you've agreed to work together. It is not a regulated industry, so while most coaches are qualified, some are not, it's up to you to ask and make the decision that's right for you.

2. What is a mentor? There are two kinds of mentors, one that gives you advice as a peer over coffee on an infrequent basis for a limited amount of time. As a sounding board, colleague, friend or friend- of-a-friend. They are usually someone who has done what you want to do either in their career or business, and can share their experiences.

The second kind of mentor is an expert who has done what you want to do, will teach you about strategies/systems you need to use to achieve your goals, working together for an agree time with their support/guidance.

It gets confusing because a Career or Business Coach listens like a coach and then gives you advice about what to do, and how to do it hence we enter the grey area of coach/mentor.

Whoever you end up working with you will achieve your goal in half the time with double the fun, for the simple reason that when you are living inside the jar you can't read the label!

Remember while much of what your coach/mentor or trainer tells you, you might know it already, it's easy to get overwhelmed, forget what you know and let yourself off the hook one too many times – remember our procrastinator archetype from earlier!

3. Do I have to pay for them? The simple answer to this questions is 'it depends'. Coaching is a profession, a Business, a job as is Training and Mentoring. Remember I mentioned two types of mentoring. I've never paid for a peer mentor and don't believe you should have to, but I have invested in coaching, training and business mentoring.

A note of caution with Coaches/Mentors/Trainers - they are your trusted adviser. You are investing in their expertise, strategies and accountability, but it is your life, your dreams, your time and what you do or don't do is your choice. Take full responsibility for your role in this partnership.

You are the CEO of your own business/career/life, you make decisions, a coach/mentor/trainer is a resource to learn to provide guidance, support and structure.

If you feel like they don't get that distinction, or that they don't seem to understand you and how you need to be supported, then terminate the relationship as soon as you can.

Trust your intuition and use it to vet everyone you work with or employ. If it doesn't feel right then it is likely that it is not right for you!

Two important things to remember:

    1. The dream/s within you.
    2. The team behind you.

You are responsible for organising and coordinating both. Surround yourself with people who have a track record, have made their own money and have finetuned their strategies.

THOUGHT PROVOCATEUR TIPS

- **Outsourcing/delegation is the ultimate key to effective time management.**

- **Invest in personal development, coaches, mentors, trainers and networks that will support your growth as a successful entrepreneur/professional and time manager.**

- **Network and attend industry and personal development events that will help you become the best version of yourself.**

CASE STUDY - Chris Paton (Executive Director, NED, Author)
www.quirksolutions.co.uk

Describe a typical working day

I am actually quite determined in not having a set routine to a day. I know that for many people having a regular rhythm to what they do really helps, but I actually find that it just gets me irritated when I inevitably can't stick to it.

Our lives are not predictable, and we often find ourselves having to deal with unexpected events, so trying to impose a standard routine is impractical.

I'd far rather adapt to each day as it comes, which makes things feel fresh and interesting. I do tend to check, before I even get up, on emails and social media for the business.

I then review the diary and see what should be prioritised for the day.

At the end of the day I try to stay off my phone within an hour of going to bed to help me relax.

Are there any times of the day that you are more effective, and if so, why do you think that's the case?

I am definitely more of a morning person and I'm most effective early on because I am rested and it fits with our natural circadian rhythms.

That said I am equally happy working in the evening and I'm perhaps more reflective at that time, whereas the morning is more of a high energy and getting tasks ticked off approach. I am definitely at my lowest point midway through the afternoon.

What distracts you from work and how do you maintain focus?

One of my biggest challenges is not having a dedicated office.

The nature of my business means that I am predominantly working at client sites, and my team do the same, so there is no justification for the overhead of an office.

As such, I find myself able to focus and produce good levels of work when I am away travelling, but when I am not, I work from a small office based in my home. This is when I am often distracted - by emails coming in, household chores, family members or the pets!

It is definitely something that I am looking to address in the near future.

What change/s have you made to increase your productivity?

Bringing an operations director into the business! Having somebody hold me to account on deliverables and timelines has really helped. I like to think that I am pretty disciplined and can focus on the tasks in hand but having that extra check and balance has been hugely beneficial.

I have also turned off notifications on emails and silenced the alerts, which means that I can stay connected to the task at hand without being interrupted by incoming messages that can be dealt with later.

Finally, I have also made a more concerted effort to find time for reflection, reading and rest. This has really helped me be more productive when I am focused on work.

What tips would you give someone that wants to improve how they spend their time?

Don't get fixated on there being a right or wrong way to structure and organise your time, work with what feels right for you.

I think it's good to listen to ideas from other people on how they organise their time and suggestions on improvements, but these don't necessarily have to become rigid guidelines or the 'right way' to do things.

I also think that, although it feels very counter intuitive and wasteful, deliberately trying to make sure you get plenty of downtime and time to reflect is very important.

Slowing down to speed up!

VOCABULARY – HOW TO TALK YOURSELF SUCCESSFUL

The language you use is creating the life you have. If there are things in your life that you want to change then it starts by learning how to talk yourself successful. The following are some common, yet negative words that are used daily, often going un-checked and yet they will unconsciously damage your effectiveness as entrepreneurs and professionals.

Should – is a hugely destructive word...

That many of us learned from our caregivers, which they learned from theirs which was then reinforced throughout education and by society.

Become aware of how much you use it by observing your language patterns for a day. Continuing to use this word in your everyday life is a habit, and something that initially you will have to work hard to break.

What does this word even mean? It refers to the expectations of others and is no longer needed in your life.

You either do or you don't, and if you need to try looking at the situation from a different perspective, understand the outcome and take charge of your life.

Shouldn't – best friends with our previous word...

How many times a day do you find yourself saying I shouldn't do...fill in the blank?

Or perhaps you hear people around you speaking about things people shouldn't do? You either will or you won't there is no should or shouldn't about the decisions you make and the actions you take.

When people are empowered to make decisions, they cease to need boundaries like this to dictate how they live their life, grow their business, progress their career.

Enough – is another expectation driven word...

Again, what does it actually mean? You either do or you don't, you can or you can't. It is up to you to decide what needs to be done and by when, to identify your requirements, look for solutions and plan your time.

In reality you will never have enough time, or money to do things, but don't let that stop you from moving forward. Trust yourself to work it out and remove this word from your vocabulary or life for that matter!

Failure – this word does not exist in my vocabulary.

There is no such thing as failure, there is an opportunity to learn from an experience and a chance to try something else.

I appreciate some of you may have business activities and job roles where there is no margin for error and failure is not an option. The failure I am talking about here is in relation to fear associated with trying something new.

To have tried and 'failed' is not a crime, to have failed to learn the lesson is the problem.

Too many people spend their whole lives hiding behind this word, afraid to give something a go because it might not work. All major innovations come from years of experimentation such as Edison and the light bulb, the Wright Brothers and powered flight – can you imagine what life would be like if they had given up?

 TIME MANAGEMENT TIP
'To be the time manager that you want to be you have to start talking to yourself like you would talk to other people'

I'm not encouraging you to run blindly into the next opportunity that comes your way, always do your research and make calculated decisions.

Fear – is a story that will keep you trapped for life if you let it.

It will convince you that you don't have time, that you aren't ready, that you shouldn't do it, you might fail and what will people think.

Below is an acronymn I use to inspire me to keep going every time I have to do something new that's outside of my comfort zone, which is daily.

Forget
Everything
And
Rise

HEALTH & LIFESTYLE

How would someone who really loved themselves look after their health and wellbeing? After my stroke I asked myself this exact question and began to change how I took care of my health, or 'the machine' as I sometimes call my body, because it helps me remember that food is fuel.

Lifestyle – Studies show that humans thrive with routine and discipline. As much as we say we hate how boring and rigid it can be, if you remove routine, you remove purpose. Box set bingeing become tedious, a week of no exercise makes you feel worse not better, and to have no purpose is to question the point to life.

It's time for some journaling, find a pen and paper and write down your answers to the following 3 questions (don't overthink it or judge yourself).

1. What kind of a lifestyle would you like?
2. Are you happy with your current lifestyle?
3. Why haven't you made changes recently?

Maybe you have tried things in the past but they haven't lasted long, we've all been there. I did a cereal diet once to drop a dress size for a holiday. For 30 days I ate 2 bowls or cereal a day plus dinner, and it worked, but it wasn't sustainable, nutritious or a demonstration of self love.

Water – drink water like your life depends on it, because it does. The average human body is around 60% water. By the time you start to feel the signs of dehydration you are actually already dehydrated. Apart from the effects it has on your body's ability to filter out toxins, it also impacts your concentration and speed of mental performance.

What tends to happen at this point is most people do not recognise it as a need for water, they think they need sugar, and so reach for a fizzy drink which gives them an instant high, and they are back to full concentration again. Look at the chart on the next page and you will see how this creates peaks and troughs, whereas water gives you a nice steady line throughout the day.

What this translates to is a 'need' for fizzy drinks to keep you going, which becomes an addiction and will account for excess weight, not to mention water actually makes your mind and your thoughts sharper than fizzy drinks do. This is not a nutrition book, if you are interested research it further. Try replacing fizzy drinks with water and see what effect it has on your daily life and productivity (you will feel funny for a day or two as your body goes cold turkey on sugar, but it won't last long).

See how much more energy you have from this simple change, not to mention more money and less weight...win-win!!

Energy fluctuations of fizzy Drinks V Water over 1 Day

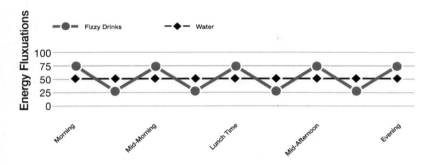

Diet – I don't mean go on one, I mean what are you eating? It is important to eat a healthy balanced diet. Replace crisps and chocolate with nuts and fruit, eat less carbohydrates (especially white bread and white pasta), eat more fruit and vegetables and recognise that your body is yours for your lifetime. You can't abuse it and then take it back to the shop for a refund or a replacement. This is your machine and it is up to you to look after it. No one else actually really cares if you are fat or thin, if getting out of bed in the morning is easy or a struggle, looking after your body is your responsibility. Taking that seriously means a mindset shift. Filling up on comfort food may make you feel good in the moment, but the key to healthy eating is balance. Of course I still eat the 'bad' foods once in a while, but now they are a treat and I allow myself to enjoy them.

With time you will get better at listening to your body. It tells you what it needs (intuitive eating), but the trouble is it only whispers, it can be hard to hear over your habits. An example might be your body whispering 'I fancy a tomato salad' (because tomatoes contain the nutrients your body may need), but your mind shouts no salad, we need chips. So you feed yourself chips with tomato ketchup and then wonder why a couple of hours later you don't feel so great. So you have a fizzy drink and welcome to the world of habit loops.

It doesn't have to be this way. Simple changes and substitutions, proper balance and careful use of treats, and you have a 'diet' that is now a life-style. Not a procession of punishments every time you need to drop a dress/trouser size, aka yo-yo diet life.

Alcohol – is a choice, it can be an enjoyable one, or it can be an escape from something. It affects everyone in a different way, by situation, type, time, frequency etc. Some people can take it or leave it, while others are addicted to it and some are functional drinkers.

I spent many years drinking to 'excess' as we all did in the 90's & 00's.

We were functional drinkers, although I always seemed to have the worst hangovers. When I started my business in 2013 I cut down to focus on growing it, then in January 2019 I quit drinking and overnight my mental health improved (no more alcohol blues), and as an added bonus I dropped a dress size and started sleeping better too.

If you resonated with this section you might want to start by reducing, or replacing alcoholic for non-alcoholic or low alcohol drinks. There are so many great substitutes out there, and experiment, it's your life!

Sleep – is a super power, it is when your body rests and repairs itself. How much you need varies from person to person (between 7-9 hours) with 7hrs 30mins being the average. A good sleep routine will help you. Keep a notebook and pen by your bedside. If you wake up in the night make a note of what is on your mind/stopping you from sleeping. This action takes the thought out of your mind, so that you can go back to sleep and address whatever you noted down with fresh energy in the morning. More about sleep on page 58.

TIME MANAGEMENT TIP
'Health is wealth, prioritise yours.'

CASE STUDY Molly Dare Hillenbrand (Founder, HillenBRAND Media, Executive Producer, Podcast Host)
www.mollydare.com

Describe a typical working day

I wake up by 6am and give myself at least 1 hour of solid me time where I am present and just do whatever I want to. It's the only hour in the day I can do this so I really look forward to it.

I'll have my coffee, sit outside with my dogs and then it's up to me to walk the dogs (we have 3), I listen to music, go on social media, read my book...whatever moves me.

Next I wake my girls take them to school and start my work day by 9am. I'll do research for upcoming interviews and then either film or record an interview segment or podcast. Followed by an hour of post interview work and head to pick up my girls from school.

From school pick up to dinner it's kid time, after dinner I usually do prep work for the following day or respond to emails. My girls and I will watch a show together before bed.

Are there any times of the day that you are more effective, and if so, why do you think that's the case?

Definitely mornings: my energy levels are at their highest as is my ability to think clearly and I am more centered so I schedule my complex tasks that need my full focus for mornings between 9am and midday.

What distracts you from work and how do you maintain focus?

Social media distracts me from work so I look at it in the afternoons or late evenings when I'm not my most focused so that I'm not wasting my most productive hours on it if I can help it!

What change/s have you made to increase your productivity?

The biggest change I've made is waking up earlier to give me that time for myself. Also giving myself the clarity of mind in the evening to identify my tasks for the next day so I can sleep well and not stay up worrying about what needs to get done.

What tips would you give someone that wants to improve how they spend their time?

Be intentional with your time and acknowledge your energy levels throughout a given day so that you can schedule and reschedule your day accordingly.

TIME CONFIDENCE

Why do you call yourself a Time Confidence Expert? the interviewer asked.

Having been a Time Management Author, Speaker, Trainer, Coach for several years I've noticed a strange phenomenon. My audiences, clients and readers didn't have time management problems, they had task management problems, which in most cases seem to stem from a lack of self-confidence.

They didn't seem to fully realise/accept that when we were talking about ways they could manage their tasks and their time, it was THEIR time we were talking about. That the strategies I was sharing really could change their careers, business, life, and improve their productivity.

They took notes, nodded, thanked me, bought my book, commented on my social media posts, some even shared them with their audiences and yet nothing was changing. There was a 'disconnect' between the information and the application of it.

TOXIC TIME MANAGEMENT

Intellectually I knew they understood what I was saying, but their lives were not improving. I knew I had done my job, I was frustrated that people were still busy, overwhelmed and burning out. Nothing seemed to be changing.

TIME MANAGEMENT TIP
"Knowledge isn't power, it's potential. When you use what you know it will change your business, career and life!"

So I did some digging and recognised a phenomenon I'd noticed in the personal development world, the 'course junkie'. A person who reads book after book, takes training after training, and sometimes doesn't finish one before starting another. They are 'Addicted' to the buzz of constantly learning new things.

I love learning, but what I love more is when things in my life improve because I apply what I've learned.

What is Toxic Time Management?   Is the addiction to knowing the latest time management hack, strategy, system, or app but not doing anything with the information. And therefore failing to be the most productive person you can be.

If you aren't using what you know - do you really know it?

THE 888 FORMULA

We all have the same 24 hours, but we don't all have the same beliefs about time. In particular the value of it, how you use yours to do one thing versus another. Was that the best ROYT (Return on Your Time)?

The 888 Formula is a cutting-edge, holistic approach to work life balance. It is a practical framework that helps individuals audit their life against 3 key metrics and identify areas for development.

1. Rest - 8 Hours
2. Activities - 8 Hours
3. Work - 8 Hours

It is the optimum way to break down a 24-hour day based on science (how much sleep the human body needs to rest & repair) and cultural norms (the hours of a working day). The Formula gives you an instant high-level snapshot of your current time allocation, and this information is the gateway to creating better work-life balance.

DO YOU IDENTIFY WITH ONE OR MORE OF THE FOLLOWING?

Are you:

1. Constantly busy
2. Easily distracted
3. Overwhelmed
4. Struggling to fit everything in
5. Uncertain about where to start
6. No idea where the time goes
7. Find it hard to remain focused
8. Always being interrupted
9. Feel unproductive
10. Frustrated
11. Looking for your purpose
12. Demotivated
13. No work/life boundaries
14. Close to burnout
15. On a hamster wheel
16. Juggling everything
17. In need of a holiday
18. Is balance even possible?

Once you understand the consequences of how you spend your time each day, whether that is feeling anxious, stressed, overwhelmed, or burnt out you will regain the power to decide what needs to change.

Just as we all have the same 24 hours, we all have the power to make changes, however big or small. We enjoy enough freedom to turn around our metaphorical car and drive it to a new destination.

8 HOURS - REST

Why do we sleep? The human body needs sleep for a variety of different reasons ranging from cell regeneration to allowing the mind to process and recalibrate the activities of the day. Moving memories from one part of the brain to another other.

When we sleep our bodies go through 4-6 sleeps cycles per night depending on how much sleep we need/how much sleep we get. A sleep cycle is divided into 4-phases and lasts around 90 minutes.

This part of the formula also looks at cutting edge research into activities like micro breaks (napping), mindfulness and meditation as forms of restorative rest.

8 BENEFITS OF SLEEP

1. During sleep our bodies rest, restore and rejuvenate, muscles grow, tissue repair, and hormones synthesize.

2. During sleep we solidify and consolidate memories from the day; information & experiences are transferred from more tentative, short-term memory to stronger, long-term memory. This process is called consolidation.

3. Cytokines, a type of protein that targets infection and inflammation, produced and released during sleep.

4. The quality of your sleep directly affects the quality of your waking life (mental & physical health).

5. Restorative sleep enables you to work, learn, create, and communicate at your full potential.

6. Making time to get the sleep you need each night means your energy, efficiency, and overall health and productivity will increase.

7. No other activity delivers so many benefits with so little effort (ROI).

8. Sleep is the rest, reset & regulation our bodies need to keep us alive!

SLEEP CYCLES

As previously mentioned when we sleep our bodies go through 4–6 sleep cycles per night depending on how much sleep we need/how much sleep we get. A sleep cycle is divided into 4–phases.

Phase 1. Non-rapid eye movement (NREM 1)

Phase 2. Non-rapid eye movement (NREM 2)

Phase 3. Non-rapid eye movement (NREM 3)

Phase 4. Rapid eye movement (REM)

When we first fall asleep we go into non–rapid eye movement sleep phase (NREM 1), at this stage we are still in light sleep and can be roused easily, there are 3 more phases like this.

At NREM 3, this is when we are in the deepest phase of the cycle, and if you were to try and wake someone up from this stage of sleep they would be disorientated and groggy. The final stage of the cycle is known as rapid eye movement sleep (REM), the stage at which people tend to dream.

A whole cycle lasts around 90 minutes and at each stage the body is working on repairing and restoring a different part of itself. To find out more I highly recommend reading *Why we Sleep*, by Matthew Walker.

See the diagram below for an illustration of what happens while you sleep.

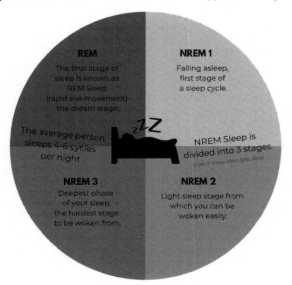

THE POWER OF NAPPING

Contrary to popular belief people who take naps are not lazy they actually understand how to recharge their energy and generate more, according to a study carried out by the School of Psychology, at Flinders University in Adelaide, Australia.

Having a 10 minute nap produced the most benefit in terms of reduced sleepiness and improved cognitive performance, but don't nap for longer than 20 minutes as the effectiveness diminishes and longer than 30 minutes can lead to grogginess and disorientation.

MICRO BREAKS & MINDFULNESS

Rest doesn't just have to be sleep. In *The Art of Rest* by Claudia Hammond she shares the results of research she carried out with 18,000 participants to better understand how people unwind, calm down and recharge.

The book covers the top 10 activities people find most restful (well worth a read), for now I will focus on micro breaks and mindfulness, Hammond quotes research that revealed 40 seconds spent looking away from a complex task at a postcard of nature improved concentration.

Were you ever told off in school for looking out of the window, when you should have been working? You were taking a micro break without even knowing it!

Mindfulness is a huge subject, and in simple terms it's any activity that brings you back to the present moment. I start most days with a mindful walk in nature, taking photos and noticing what's around me, the colours, the shapes, the types of animal, the bird song and the sounds.

If you don't have time/are unable to leave your desk. Look away from your screen and, notice the things in the room around you, the colours the shapes, the temperature of the room, what can you smell?

Close your eyes, breathe in through your nose and out through your mouth three times, drink some water and get back to work. I am a huge convert to Breathwork and recommend that you look into it for energy and meditation/mindful benefits. Always consult a medical doctor if you're unsure whether something is right for you.

MEDITATION

Meditation is a type of mindful activity that relaxes your nervous system, moving it from fight and flight mode, into rest and digest.

When I meditation I sit on a chair and focus on my breathing (for 8-minutes) allowing my thoughts to float past like clouds, it takes practice and some days are easier then others. I also remind myself that even though the results may not be immediately visible, something beneficial has happened.

There are many styles of meditation and you may feel too busy to do it, but the science is there to support the health benefits. Do some research and find something that works for you – use how you feel as your guide.

8 HOURS - ACTIVITIES

This part of the formula covers everything an individual does on a daily basis that isn't related to Rest or Work, it is the jam in the 888 sandwich.

People are shocked when they realise that these 8 hours are divided between time spent food shopping, cooking and eating, washing of all kinds (clothes and body) beauty and skincare routines, and the house work. Time for family and relationships, personal time to journal/read/exercise, time with pets. Time to manage personal/life admin, time to study and attend networking and training courses and events.

As well as time for hobbies, your daily commute and let's not forget time for Netflix and relaxing.

THE WORK LIFE/BALANCE MYTH

Think of someone you admire, you have the same 24 hours as they do. Granted you may not have their parents, their intelligence, their bank balance, or their entourage, but get excited for a minute you DO have the same amount of time as they do each day, and unless they inherited their wealth, they have been where you are.

Which by my calculations means if it is possible for them, then it is possible for you too!

Whether the glass is half empty or half full is irrelevant.

SUCCESS MINDSET

Do you want to believe that if you knew what they did, had similar habits and mindset to them and took different actions to the ones you do today, then things in your life could change? Maybe not immediately but do you believe that change is possible?

Success mindset is a choice, you don't have to think optimistically, but if you can change the way you look at things, then the life experience you are having will change.

Habits are soft-wired in our brains, they are learnt behaviour that can be unlearned, and reprogrammed. Our brains are 'plastic' and recent scientific discoveries in the field of neuroscience show that contrary to their previous understanding of how the brain worked - new neural pathways continue to be made in our brain throughout our lives.

It was believed that plasticity could only happened in the brains of children up to a certain age, but it turns out that our brains continue to learn and evolve until we die (you can teach an old dog new tricks as the saying goes) so it's never too late!

RETURN ON YOUR TIME

How you invest your time, is creating the reality you are experiencing as you read this book right now.

Your life experience to date is the culmination of the things you have been doing and continue to do day in day out.

Back on that cold February morning in 2012 the only thoughts I remember having in the moments I believed I was going to die were regret. That I'd never truly lived, that I'd spent 99.9% of my time and my life doing what I thought I should be doing and 0.1% doing what I wanted to do and then feeling guilty about it for ages after.

So I begged the powers that be for another chance and I promised that I'd spend my second chance sharing this message with the world.

Make every minute count.

Before that day I didn't know life could be different, that there was other way of doing things. Everyone I knew was doing it the way I was doing it.

Personal development wasn't what it is now. The Internet, Google, YouTube, Instagram weren't what they are today. Inspirational books were few and far between, no one was sharing their success tips or f**k up stories and mobile phones were for calls and text messages only.

TIME MANAGEMENT TIP
'Don't regret the decision you didn't make, chances you didn't take, and life you didn't live '

These days you can find answers to your questions at the click of a button. Every day another piece of history is being re told and new role models are stepping into the light.

This pillar of the Formula can be anything you want it to be. We over estimate what we can achieve in a day, and fail to appreciate our lives are a marathon not a sprint.

WHAT DO YOU WANT?

Dare to dream. Use this section as your opportunity to name the things you want to change and commitment to do whatever it takes to stick to your decision. This is your life.

TIP – Visit <u>www.successbydesigntraining.com</u> to find out about the training, workshops and experts we've partnered with to bring you the solutions to your problems.

8 HOURS - WORK

For the last few hundred years society has traditionally operated a 5-day week with an 8 hour working day model. In recent years some industries and sectors have adopted a more flexible approach to work based on the premise that 'as long as the work is done' then the logistics are up to you.

All training in this area of the formula focuses on sharing tips, tools and strategies you can use to improve your productivity, working smarter, not harder.

STRUCTURE YOUR DAY

Whether you take 8-hours to complete your daily activities or 12 hours to do 8 hours of work the choice is yours.

Gone are the days of long hours for the sake of it. Being busy is not a badge of honour it's a red flag.

If you're working for a visionary organisation you will probably know much of what I am about to share. Keep reading.

Whether you run your own business or support people in an organisation productivity matters.

Time is finite, decisions about resource allocation need to be constantly reassessed, you can't reclaim what's lost but you can stop wasting what you have.

Is this my top priority?

Is a question that you must ask yourself regularly The world changes fast and it's not slowing down any time soon.

How you spend your time matters, it's either building and growing a business or organisation, or it's being wasted on low value tasks or non urgent priorities, and as time machines don't exist (yet) it can't be recovered.

The ability to continually evaluate and respond is a skill worth developing.

WORK FUNDS DREAMS

Our training teaches professionals and business owners how to improve their productivity and maximise time.

'When you love what you do you'll never work another day in your life'. It can be quite annoying to hear people say things like that, if what you do can also be stressful at times. Once you have a plan and you practice it daily you will notice improvements. You were born to live, not to spend all your time working, no matter how much you might love what you do. Get your balance back and you'll get your life back.

No one ever died saying they wished they had worked longer hours!

8 STEPS TO BECOME A CONFIDENT TIME MANAGER

1. It's my time

2. I decide how to organise my to do list

3. I am flexible and able to respond quickly when things change

4. I take responsibility for completing my tasks on time

5. I ask for help when I need it

6. I resist procrastination because I hate feeling stuck

7. I get my work done during my contracted hours

8. I feel confident saying no to speculative requests

ENERGY MANAGEMENT

While our time is finite our energy is rechargeable. Below are activities I do on a daily basis to ensure I stay and perform at my optimum all day long.

We call it the 8-Minute Secret and the activities fall under 3 pillars:

1. Movement

2. Mindset

3. Meditation

Each pillar has its own activities and we recommend you try them and interchange until you find a routine that works for you.

TIP – Visit   www.successbydesigntraining.com for more information about our 8-Minute Secret training and find out how you can use simple 8-minute activities to reset your energy throughout the day.

TIME PLANNING

WHAT A STANDARD WORKING WEEK COULD LOOK LIKE:

The following chart helps you to understand how you can get more hours from a standard working week. Obviously it goes without saying that your working day may start earlier and end later, there is no one size fits all. Sleep requirements, roles and responsibilities, are all different. You have to find what works for you, create your formula and the work/life balance you want, and enjoy experimenting.

Week	06.00-09.00	09.00-12.00	12.00-13.00	13.00-17.00	17.00-22.00	Total
	3hrs	Work	1hr	Work	5hrs	7hrs x 5days = 35hrs work
						9hrs x 5days = 45hrs free
Weekend	06.00				22.00	Total
						16hrs x 2 days = 32hrs free

Self	Job	Family/Friends/Social
Home, leisure, hobbies	Work, business, projects	Partner, family, children
41 hours	35 hours	41 hours
1/3 of your time	1/3 of your time	1/3 of your time

45 hrs + 32 hrs = 77 hours free per week

35 hrs work

In the tables above you have an example of what is possible when you start breaking down your 24-hour day. You will find that you have more time than you realised. The time you go to bed up is your choice, as is how much sleep you need, how long you take for lunch and how many hours you work each day. Once you start managing your time more efficiently you will have more for yourself, your family, friends and relationships.

Of course life doesn't always go to plan. There will be times when you need more sleep, or when work, or your family requires more focus. But if you keep this example in the back of your mind it will help you to remember that you control your time and it doesn't control you. Balance is the result of the decisions you make and the actions you take. That really is the key to happiness.

You will never look at time in the same way again. Every decision you make will have a different meaning. You will carry out a mental assessment before you say yes to invitations, extra work or client projects. You will see outsourcing and delegation for the time freedom it brings you both at work and home.

TIME MANAGEMENT TIP
'Activities can tend to take as long to execute as the amount of time that you allow for them to be completed in'

MINDSET

Work on your mindset, practice it daily. In previous sections I recommended that you read books, attend workshops and online training. Feed your mind with positivity, possibility and proof of what's possible.

Once you finish this book and start making changes in your life, you will encounter resistance from yourself and others. If change were easy everyone would have the lifestyle they want. Knowing what to change is simple, but making the changes is not so simple because you will have to leave your comfort zone, the familiar, the people you know and the results you have - in order to achieve the results you want.

You will need to create a tool kit of positivity that you use on a daily basis to ensure you are in control of your mind, and it's not controlling you.

Create a morning routine that includes at least 8 minutes of one of the following meditation, journaling, walking, yoga flow or reading. These activities are taken from our 8-minute secret program, that teaches you how to create a self-care routine that suits you.

In the years that followed my stroke I realised that in my pursuit of the perfect life, career, handbag, party or holiday I'd neglected the most important part of the whole equation.

Me: my health, my wellbeing and my diet. Everything was last minute, quick fixes, skipped meals and little or poor sleep.

TIP – Visit www.successbydesigntraining.com for more information about our 8-Minute Secret training and find out how you can use simple 8-minute activities to reset your energy throughout the day.

TIME MANAGEMENT TIP
*'Be a dream chaser, chase your own dreams
not somebody else's'*

You can have whatever you want in life, the question is how much do you want it? And are you willing to do whatever it takes to achieve it?

You decide. The actions you are currently taking are creating the work, business, life you currently have.

If you want things to be different then you will need to try new things. You can't reap what you don't sow.

Every time you find your mind taking a walk down negativity alley, talking about the past or worrying about the future stop and ask yourself this simple question, am I being present?

Everything that happens to you is actually happening for you, to teach you the lessons you most need to learn, in order to become the person you came here to be.

It doesn't negate what has happened, but finding a way to make peace with it will set you free. In most cases it will require professional support - research CBT, EMDR, Hypnotherapy. Accepting that my stroke happened for me took some time to get my head around, but if I hadn't had it, it's unlikely you would be reading this book!

By accepting that what happened to me, happened for me I have been able make peace with myself, and the situation and start making the most of the second chance I have. Looking forward at what I can achieve with it and not back at what my life once was.

GET ORGANISED

Take control of your time, get organised and you will be amazed at how much more time you are able to create on a daily weekly, monthly, yearly basis.

There is enough time for you to get all of the important things done!

The problem is you will have to stop the 'busy work' for long enough to see that not only is it stealing your time, it's keeping you trapped. Your mind has convinced you that what you are doing is the best thing to be doing, but if you were doing something else then you would have a next level life.

"What we fear doing most is usually what we most need to do"
Tim Ferriss

8 THINGS TO DO DAILY TO GET MORE ORGANISED

The following is a list of activities you can try to get more organised on a daily basis, focus on trying one at a time.

I suggest you start with number 8 first and work backwards, getting the sleep your body needs is the foundation for lasting change.

1. **Alarm Time** - What time does your alarm go off? Try using an alarm that wakes you up at the end of a sleep cycle (you can find more info about this on our website).

2. **Morning routine** - As discussed previously the 8- Minute Secret helps you create a self-care routine from as little as 8 minutes a day.

3. **What time do you start work?** - Having a fixed start time will give your day structure, especially if you are working from home, without the social cues of the office to guide you. Create a routine that works for you and the job/business requirements you have.

4. **Take a lunch break** - Looking after your health is your responsibility. You can't help anyone else if you don't. It's your wealth and needs to be a priority, especially if you run your own business, can you afford to be sick? Taking breaks will make you more productive, not less.

5. **What time do you finish work?** - Just like point 3 knowing when you finish means you'll be less inclined to procrastinate. Boundaries like these will help you prevent burnout, and improve your productivity.

6. **Dinner time routine** - Like point 4 prioritising when you eat, what you eat, and how you prepare your food is less about necessity and more a demonstration of self-love.

7. **Evening routine/s** - Without a plan for your evening it's easy to either carry on working, zone out in front of the TV or a box set, or scroll the time away on social media.

8. **Bed time routine** - How much sleep you need will dictate everything, once you know that you can work back, it takes the average person 15 mins to fall asleep so factor that into the time your lights go out.

THOUGHT PROVOCATEUR TIP

- **Learn how to talk to yourself successfully and filter unhelpful negative words out of your vocabulary.**

- **Look after your body, you only get one and the success of your business is tied to the health of it.**

- **Recognise that you have more time than you might have realised and start taking control.**

- **Understand that if you improve your mindset then your life and success of your business/career will benefit beyond belief.**

- **Create a routine that works for you and your life, which of the 8 things will you try doing daily to get more organised?**

- **Organisation is the key to effective time management, start taking control of the time you are now reclaiming and start planning.**

CASE STUDY Darrell Evans (Founder, CEO, Podcast Host)
www.darrellevans.net

Describe a typical working day

The typical day starts between 5:30-6:00am without an alarm clock unless I have a plane to catch.

My morning routine starts by drinking 16 ounces of room temperature water. I'll often include freshly squeezed lemon juice. This helps me rehydrate after a night of sleep.

Next, I meditate for 10-20 mins. Using guided meditations as well as music and sound meditations (Insight Timer app). Breath of Fire, a Kundalini yoga technique is one of my favourites. It clears any groggy energy I may have from dreams or sleep. After meditating, I typically read the day's scripture from my Bible app and pray.

Then I stretch for about 10 minutes while listening to something motivational or inspirational. I like to stretch my upper and lower back hamstrings and calves because I work at a computer. Foam rollers and resistance bands are my best friends.

I'll then begin thinking about my schedule for the day, my goals for the week or quarter. Coffee is usually next. I check email around 7-7:30 am and am only looking for something urgent to stand out.

Otherwise, I put it away until I'm ready to process it. Processing is a David Allen technique (Getting Things Done) I've been using for almost 20 years. By following this routine more often than not, I have a strong foundation for the scheduled and unscheduled happenings of the day.

Are there any times of the day that you are more effective, and if so, why do you think that's the case?

I love the morning and mid-day hours before 2 pm. I used to work a lot at night and call myself a night owl and say I did my best work then. This led to working round the clock, depriving my body of sleep, and experiencing burnout.

I've learned that my best work is when I decide to plan and schedule my best work. I also believe that we do our best work when our work matches our Superstar DNA (Definite Natural Ability).

When I have projects that align with my natural ability versus one I've adapted to or learned due to responsibility, I perform both effectively and efficiently.

What distracts you from work and how do you maintain focus?

If I'm honest, everything distracts me. I'm human and grateful to be living in such extraordinary times. I love the connection from social media, email, and tech. I love the ability to listen to podcasts and audio books while at the gym or driving.

It's happened more often than I'd like to admit where time has flown by without me realising. To help avoid distractions, and remain focused I schedule almost everything. If it matters, it's in my calendar (family time, vacations, date night, self-care, projects & meetings).

Doing this my team can see how I spend my time each week, which means that I can lead by example.

What change/s have you made to increase your productivity?

The biggest change I've made to increase my productivity has been respecting sleep. For almost all of my thirties, I'd burn the midnight oil and get 4-6.5 hours a night. In my forties, that changed and I'm committed to getting seven hours per night.

That meant going to bed earlier. Today, that is between 9-10pm most weekday nights. I wind down before bed by listening to a sleep music meditation to help me calm my mind and prepare me for sleep.

This has been a game-changer for me. I also started monitoring my sleep patterns by wearing my Fitbit to bed. I admit it felt odd at first to wear a watch to bed. I love seeing what my sleep was like the night before. If you can track it, you can improve it if you want to.

What tips would you give someone that wants to improve how they spend their time?

The first tip is to get clear on the personal and business outcomes you want to create or manifest in your life.

Then, make your decisions fall into one of three buckets below:

1. Hell Yes
2. Hell No
3. Maybe (means "no" unless something changes)

The "hell yes" distinction changes how you see a time commitment.

Anything you say "yes" to is a "no" to something else.

There is an opportunity cost to every time commitment you make.

If you're a high achiever like me, then you've been guilty of saying yes to everything in the past too!

Then realising you've buried yourself in commitments.

"Hell yes" draws a line in the emotional sand and reduces the weight of the commitments you make.

There's power in saying no.

In some cases you're not saying no because you don't want to do it.

You're saying no because it will infringe other commitments that were a "hell yes."

If it is a "Hell Yes" then, get it in your calendar.

QUESTIONS

As a child I asked a lot of questions, most started with the word 'why', and initially my curiosity was indulged by whoever I asked (everyone I met). Then as I got older I was discouraged from asking so many questions, and encouraged to accept that this was just how thing were. As a result I got out of the habit of asking them, and started to accept that how things were must be normal. Maybe you experienced the same?

Then one day I noticed I had started asking questions again, only this time they were disempowering questions like:

- Why does this always happen to me?
- What did I do to deserve this?
- Why can't I ever seem to get things right?

"I can not teach anybody anything, I can only make them think"
Socrates

I had moved from curiosity about the world around me to an obsessive desire to understand what I was doing wrong and why I wasn't experiencing the same success as others.

Having immersed myself in the personal development world since my stroke I now understand that the quality of our questions dictates our results.

Now I am able to adapt my actions or responses to life events by asking an empowering question like what can I learn from this?

I regularly come back to Habit 5 in Stephen Covey's book *The 7 Habits of Highly Effective People*. 'Seek first to understand then be understood'.

Don't ever stop asking questions, beware of the empowering or disempowering nature of them - don't let your own mind be your worst enemy!

ACTION PLAN

So far you have assessed how you spend your time, identified where you waste it and made an agreement with yourself to start making necessary changes. You also now understand how much power outsourcing and delegation can give you in terms of turning your time into productivity.

"The journey of a thousand miles begins with a single step."
Lao Tzu

Now it is time to start setting goals and creating your own personal action plan so you can begin making your dream life your real life.

GOAL SETTING

In order to set goals for the future it is important to identify what it is that you want from your life, who you are, what you enjoy doing, and what you are good at.

Set aside some time to sit quietly on your own in a comfortable place where you can relax and allow your mind to wander off to a time one year from now.

- See what you see
- Hear what you hear
- Smell what you smell
- Taste what you can taste
- Feel what you can feel

Where are you? Who are you with? Can you tell what country or location you are in? What are you eating or drinking? What are you wearing, can you feel the material? What can you hear, birds, sea, wind, traffic?

Make a note of what you can see/hear/smell/taste/touch. Be as detailed as possible, so that when you have achieved it you can look back and notice how much of what you are visualising today has become your reality. You can re-read it on the days when you are struggling with motivation, it will help you keep going.

Make a note of how you are feeling in the future; are you happy, relaxed, in control, on the way to attaining the financial and work freedom that you desire? How does it feel? If you had to give the feeling a colour what would that colour be? Write that down as well.

This exercise is designed to help you to tap into your inner wisdom. Change is a rollercoaster, there will be times when it might feel like you want to go back to what you know – but stick with it, changing old habits takes time. There has never been a better time to step into your power, and become the confident entrepreneur and professional you always have been.

Any discomfort you feel is an indication that what you are doing is having an effect and that you are getting somewhere, some people call these feelings 'growing pains'.

Grow through them and evolve into the best version of yourself!

"In order to do something that you have never done, you need to become someone that you have never been"
Les Brown

Some people talk about faking it till you make it, and others say you must act as if. For me it's a combination of both, combined with finding your inner courage and the reasons why you want things to change, then keeping them close to hand.

You really are much stronger than you know, and it is only when you're truly tested that you will realise just how strong you are. All the answers are inside you, and trust me whatever gets thrown your way you will handle it. What doesn't kill you only make you stronger!

By stepping into your true power, you will change everything around you. Your new energy will attract different things, new doors will open, and miracles will happen.

When you step into your power, you become the person you were always meant to be.

"Character isn't something you were born with and can't change, like your fingerprints. It's something you weren't born with and must take responsibility for forming"
Jim Rohn

Now it's time to set some goals, if you know about the SMART goal setting method then use that.

What will being more time confident mean for your business/career/life?

Become an action taker and start taking back control of your time and life.

Take Control

Imagine your future

Manage your time

Evaluate your successes

Questions to consider when goal setting - For the purposes of this exercise, keep your goal setting focused on becoming more Time Confident. This exercise can be applied to all areas of your life, but we are not focusing on those areas right now, one step at a time!

At first it will feel uncomfortable because you are creating new habits and this is to be expected. However if this feeling continues then create a new goal that works for you.

You may not get things right the first time; it is not a failure it is an opportunity to learn, and keep moving forward. As I said earlier I see failure as feedback, and proof that I am courageous enough to try new things.

TIME MANAGEMENT TIP
'Winners always find a way!'

When you set your goals, make it something you will do to take control of your time.

Imagine the future you will create from the new actions you take and then take them.

Try your new habits on for size, until one day they become second nature.

Don't forget we over estimate what we can achieve in a day and under estimate what we can achieve in a week, month or year.

List five outcomes that you want in your life from being an effective time manager.

1. ....

2. ....

3. ....

4. ....

5. ....

Now take your five things and arrange them in the table below in order of priority. One example is there for your reference. To get a blank document go to our website and download one – keep it on your desk or close to hand and for daily reference.

What do you want to achieve	When do you want to achieve it by	How you will achieve it
Effective time management	Within 3 months	Prioritise activities, outsource non-core skill set

TIP – Visit our <u>website</u> to download a hard copy of the table that you can complete by hand.

Becoming more time confident will open up a world of possibility for you, as you will now have the time to be, do and have.

TIME MANAGEMENT TIP
'Make your reasons for change big enough that it matters whether or not you actually make changes'

TIP – Visit our <u>website</u> to download a hard copy of the courage acronym and refer to it when you need to make tough decisions.

Something to remember: making changes takes...

Creativity: Think outside the box and look for new solutions to everyday challenges.

Options: Regularly review all your options, they will change as you do.

Universal: Be aware of the world around you; who says you need to reinvent the wheel? Make time to broaden your knowledge.

Rare: You are unique, there is no one else in this world like you with your vision and determination; take time to appreciate the value of your skills and abilities.

Action: So what if you have never done it before, 99.9% of your peers are in the same boat – give it a go, and learn every lesson and adapt as necessary.

Gauge: This is your business, your career, review and amend as necessary and if you don't have the answers find people that do, or outsource or delegate it.

Excellence: The culmination of having courage, your new way of living; live with a drive for excellence, remember you get to define what excellence means to you and your business or career!

"Winners never quit and quitters never win"
Vince Lombardi

RESET METHOD

In my work with clients a consistent pattern has emerged, they all over estimated what they could achieve during the time we worked together.

The Reset Method was born, to support their success, a 5-Step Framework, that went on to become the 25 Day Reset Program, one of our most popular and successful group programs.

TIP – Visit our <u>website</u> to join the waitlist and get notified when we run the next one.

This section of the journey is where you have to dig deep inside yourself. I know how tempting it is to put the book down and say 'that was an interesting read' and carry on as before. I know because I have a large collection of books – don't let it become shelf-development.

What we are working on here is very different it is self development. Don't let your internal resistance beat you into a corner of inaction. You clearly wanted to get more time, which is why you bought the book. You owe it to yourself to do the exercises, to try out a new way of living and see how it work for you!

I challenge you to take on the tasks in life that scare you the most, because these are the activities that you will learn the best lessons from, and life is all about learning.

VISION BOARD

Do you have a vision board? If not, now is a great time to make one.

It is a collection of images, quotes and words that sum up the lifestyle you dream of having.

Include pictures of the homes and cars you'd like to have, countries you want to visit, and clothes you would like to wear. As well as words that describe your life and the emotions you want to be feeling.

It should be a reflection of the lifestyle that you want to have, a clear vision of what it is that you are aiming for. I know people who include pictures of people who inspire them, photographs of their families and friends, or mentors, the list is endless, and you don't just have to do one vision board you can have a few.

It is an activity that is personal to you, and there is more information about how to create one on our website, along with examples. A vision board can be physical (made up of cuttings) or virtual (created on the Internet) but the point of it is that it should act as inspiration, a road map for where you are going in your life and your business journey, and career plans. It is something that you review regularly to remind yourself of what you have achieved, where it is that you are going, and why you are doing it in the first place. It should give you inspiration to keep going!

TIP – Visit our website www.successbydesigntraining.com for more information about vision boards and examples for your reference.

THOUGHT PROVOCATEUR TIPS

- Use questions to empower your learning and help you to take charge of your life, your time and your success.

- Set goals that incorporate all of your new discoveries about time management from the book, specify when you want to achieve them by and what you will do to ensure that you achieve them – keep this document close to hand and review it regularly.

- Print out the courage acronym and commit to reading it at least once a week to remind yourself of the things that you need to consider when it comes to making changes in your whole life as a result of reading this book.

- Spend time creating a vision board either online or a hard copy and look at it regularly to remind yourself of why you are doing what you are doing.

- Most importantly TAKE ACTION!

BONUS: PROFESSIONAL TIME TIPS

"Regularly define tasks that can be delegated and delegate them to the right persons."

Julia Schmidt
www.linkedin.com/in/juliaschmidtea

"I utilise Microsoft Office Tasks. I can view it at the same time as my emails. Everything in one place almost like command control."

Paula Harding
www.linkedin.com/in/paulaaharding

"Managing my inbox (and my leaders) is crucial for me in making best use of our time. I follow the 4 D's system"

Alice Scutchey
www.linkedin.com/in/alicescutchey

"For me it's being self-disciplined with time and knowing when to say "no". I allow myself to set healthy boundaries both professional and personal to protect my time, energy, creativity, and emotional well-being."

Hettle Vasani
www.linkedin.com/in/hettle-vasani

"I love using the Pomodoro technique, focusing on ONE task at a time for 25 mins and then taking a break before focusing on the next one. Breaking down bigger projects into smaller tasks, is a great way to get a quick win and provides a feeling of achievement and motivation to tackle the next thing on the list."

Karima Akil
www.linkedin.com/in/karima-akil

"My energy levels are crucial to my work. My mind, body and soul really need to be fed, watered and exercised before I start my day. I've taken time to learn what that means for me, and use it to elevate my vibration. Finding what works is personal, enlightening and an important part of our journey."

Lorraine Bellamy
www.linkedin.com/in/lorraine-bellamybwl

BONUS: ENTREPRENEUR TIME TIPS

"Hire an exceptional assistant."

As entrepreneur Jeff Hoffman says 'If you don't have an assistant, you are an assistant'.

How much is your time worth an hour? An exceptional assistant will give you back up to 80% of your time by handling all the task-based, administrative detail, process and procedure, leaving you freed up to do the things that you are exceptional at. For months when I first started my business, I argued with myself about whether I could afford it. Once I hired Matt, I realised that I couldn't afford not to. It revolutionised my business.

Lucy Brazier
www.executivesupportmedia.com

"My morning routine helps me start the day in a peak state of focus, flow and positivity."

Pepita Soler
www.pepitassecretariesclub.com

"I spend 15 mins at the end of each day planning for the next day, I use MS OneNote from Microsoft to keep track of my task list."

Helen Monument
www.monumentalassistance.com

"Time Management is a discipline that you can use to create a life of opportunity."

Skevi Constantinou
www.thepaway.co.uk

"Use a task management app like Trello or Asana to get everything out of you head. Doing this helps me keep track of my priorities, so I always know what I need be working on next without having to rewrite my to do list 50 times a day."

Laura Bradley
www.jointheofficials.com

"Take regular meaningful breaks away from your screen. Go for a walk, even if it is to the kitchen to make a cup of tea. Regular breaks really help with procrastination and you will find you can focus on what you need to achieve with much more clarity after a break."

Nicky Christmas
www.practicallyperfectpa.com

BONUS: ENTREPRENEUR TIME TIPS CONTINUED

"Having multiple businesses makes the management of my time essential. I plan my time weekly in this order and have a few fundamentals that are non negotiable for me.

1. First I block out time in my diary for "life areas" family, fitness, hobbies and self education. These are always added first!

2. Then I block time for my key revenue generating activities.

3. Next I allocate half day blocks of time to each of my businesses.

4. Finally I block time for non-revenue generating activities and tasks such as phone calls or admin for those businesses.

These principles help me focus on what's important and allow all areas of my life to flourish."

Paul Abercrombie
www.PaulAbercrombie.club

"Anything that's been in my to do list for 2 weeks I remove, as it's obviously not a priority. Replace when it becomes a priority."

Carrie Moss
www.militarymatchmaker.co.uk

"Physical maintenance is one of the most important factors of self care for me. It puts me in a sharper state of mind, which allows for more productivity in my day"

Christian Alozie
www.castalentagency.com

"I've had a morning routine for years. I keep it simple and it guarantees I begin my day in peak state. I wake up at 6am, start with 15 mins of meditation, visualisation and intention setting for the day, have a big drink of water (500ml-1L), move my body, in the gym weightlifting or on a long beach walk with Neville my dog"

Sharada Weil
www.blondeandstrong.com

"If you are working hard into the night, sometimes it's best to step away, get some shut eye and return with fresh eyes and a well rested mind. Tiredness can result in mistakes that will cost you even more time, stress and money."

Greg Lennox
www.greatzeus.co.uk

ACKNOWLEDGEMENTS

Thank you to everyone who has supported me in my journey to make this revised and updated book a reality.

I can't wait to hear how it helps support you on your journey to becoming a time confident entrepreneur and professional!

Huge thanks to my wonderful and amazing parents whose unconditional love and limitless support is something that I will be eternally grateful for.

Big thanks to my sister and brother for believing in and supporting me with your encouraging words of wisdom and love.

Special thanks to my new sister-in-law Charlotte for being such a wonderful cheerleader, and to my amazing new brother-in-law Greg for his graphic design skills, revising and updating the cover!

Thanks to the rest of my gorgeous family, love to you all.

Thanks to my childhood BFF Helen Austin-Smith, her husband Darren and beautiful family for your unwavering support and enthusiasm in my project, and to all my amazing friends around the world both new and old.

Finally I would like to thank, you the reader, for supporting and inspiring me to create the revised and updated version of my previous book. I can't wait to hear from you.

CASE STUDY BIOGRAPHIES

Suzanne Shaw

Singer, Actress, Entrepreneur

www.thehappyhealthclub.com

Singer, actress and TV personality Suzanne Shaw, became a member of the chart-topping band Hear'say in 2001, selling over 1.5 million records, holding a world record for the fastest selling non-charitable single.

She won series 3 of 'Dancing on Ice', was series regular Eve Jenson in the popular UK soap opera Emmerdale and has numerous West End and touring theatre credits.

At the start of 2020, Suzanne completely changed her lifestyle. She quit drinking, went plant-based, took up running and studied nutrition and mindfulness.

Determined to change the perception of mental health, Suzanne documented an honest account of her journey through her online platforms and was overwhelmed by the response from her audience and the media.

This was the catalyst for launching her online wellness platform, 'The Happy Health Club' a community for people to enjoy learning more about the benefits of nutrition, movement and mindfulness without being overwhelmed with crazy goals, fad diets or too much information.

Dr Lynda Shaw

Neuroscientist, Author, Speaker

www.drlyndashaw.com

Dr Lynda Shaw is an enthusiastic and engaging speaker who delights audiences around the world.

She is an experienced entrepreneur having owned 3 businesses and holds a doctorate in cognitive neuroscience, specialising in unconscious processing of emotion and behavioural change.

She is an applied cognitive neuroscientist, business psychologist and National President of the Professional Speaking Associated UK&I.

One of her specialties is communication virtually or in person and she delights in sharing her knowledge to facilitate behavioural change in the workplace.

She works with senior leaders and their teams who want to better understand the science of change and development and harness this power through heightened awareness of how their brain works, limiting beliefs and how to take charge of one's behaviour for the better in this fast-changing world.

She is founder of the Neuroscience Professional Development Programme and The Learning Lab designed to help professional people use applied neuroscience in their work. Lynda's work is always informative, fun and extremely practical.

In addition to being a neuroscientist and business person she's also great fun!

Chris Paton

Executive Director, NED, Author

www.quirksolutions.co.uk

Chris is the Executive Director of Quirk Solutions, a consultancy specialising in the human factors behind change, transformation and risk.

Clients include Lloyd's Corporation, Waitrose, Shell, Unilever, Linklaters, Mercedes and the UK National Health Service (NHS).

Chris is a recognised leader in the field of gaming, transformation & change and has delivered consultancy to a wide range of public and private sector organisations. He has lectured at the London Business School Executive Education programme, and has delivered keynote speeches in New York, Berlin, London, Glasgow, Manchester and Cannes. Published in the Harvard Business Review in 2010 with an article on managing complex and uncertain situations, Chris has also had an article in Strategy Magazine in 2018, and Business Continuity Magazine.

In his former career, Chris was a Lieutenant Colonel in the Royal Marines and advisor to the Cabinet and National Security Council on the Afghan strategy. He saw active service in a wide range of places including Northern Ireland, Kosovo, Georgia and Afghanistan. His most senior role saw him as Head of Afghan Strategy to the David Cameron Government, where he was responsible for overseeing the strategy to extract all UK combat troops and their equipment in a 2-year timeframe. This was one of the largest strategic initiatives the UK had undertaken for over 60 years.

A fluent French speaker with a Masters Degree in International Liaison and Communication, Chris is a Fellow of the Strategic Planning Society as well as a Fellow of the Society of Leadership Fellows, St George's House.

He is a proud father and husband, and someone who tries to correct his many faults as best he can - but recognises that is an ongoing project!

Molly Dare Hillenbrand

Founder, HillenBRAND Media, Executive Producer, Podcast Host

www.mollydare.com

Known for her powerhouse PR skills, Molly Dare Hillenbrand founded hillenBRAND Media in 2017, promoting entrepreneurs, business owners and media personalities through filmed social media segments, on-camera interviews, and podcast episodes of On Air with Molly Dare.

Molly is also known for her work both in front of, and behind, the camera. She has hosted and produced multiple nationwide segments for the 'Eye On' channel, providing viewers with insight happenings in their city, while simultaneously giving brands exposure to viewers across the country.

Molly's incredible work ethic has kept her at the top of her field year after year most recently being featured on the cover of Formidable Woman Magazine and a sought after guest on numerous podcasts.

Undoubtedly, Molly's most important role in life (and biggest passion!) is being a single mom to her two talented and beautiful daughters, Carolyn and Sophie, and her three super cute and snuggly dogs.

Darrell Evans

Co-Founder, Entrepreneur, Host of the MindShift Podcast

www.themindshiftpodcast.com
www.mindshiftbusinessacademy.com
www.darrellevans.net
www.yokellocal.com

Darrell Evans is a successful multi-passionate entrepreneur, with over two decades worth of experience. He is a business growth strategist and host of The MindShift Podcast, where he interviews inspirational guest sharing their stories as well and his tips, tricks and strategies to help you shift your mindset and change your life, he is also the creator of the MindShift Academy.

"You're just one SHIFT away from the breakthrough you've been looking for"

As the Co-founder of YokelLocal, an inbound marketing growth agency, he and his team have helped their clients generate over $300M in revenue online since 2011.

ABOUT THE AUTHOR

Abigail Barnes is the founder of Success by Design Training, an award-winning entrepreneur, author, speaker, and corporate trainer on time management and productive wellbeing. She is a qualified coach and creator of the renowned 888 Formula.

Success by Design Training is on a mission to share The 888 Formula with 1 million people by 2025, helping entrepreneurs & professionals find their way to reclaim an hour a day and improve their work/life balance!

TRAINING & ENQUIRIES

At Success by Design Training we work with ambitious Professionals, Entrepreneurs and Organisations that want to take control of their time and become the most productive person they know, with the work/life balance they want, doing less not more.

We Offer: Self-Study Programs, 1:1 Coaching, Online Group Programs, Workshops, Consulting Services and Keynote Speaking.

Book Abigail to speak: All talks and training are bespoke tailored to your event agenda, training requirements and audience. They can be delivered in person, online or hybrid.

For training visit: www.successbydesigntraining.com
Email: enquiries@successbydesigntraining.com

STAY SOCIAL

For daily motivation & inspiration connect with Abigail on:

Instagram: @abarnesauthor
Twitter: @abarnesauthor
Facebook: @abarnesauthor
Pinterest: @abarnesauthor
Clubhouse: @abarnesauthor

YouTube: Abigail Barnes
Linkedin: Abigail Barnes